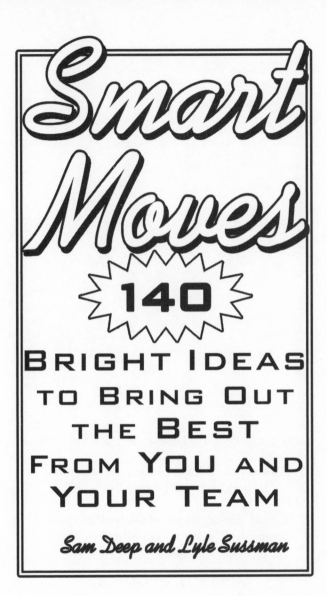

Smart Moves

140

BRIGHT IDEAS TO BRING OUT THE BEST FROM YOU AND YOUR TEAM

Sam Deep and Lyle Sussman

BARNES & NOBLE BOOKS
NEW YORK

2004 Barnes & Noble Books

ISBN 0-7607-6262-7

Printed and bound in the United States of America

04 05 06 07 08 09 MC 9 8 7 6 5 4 3 2 1

CONTENTS

2

Deliver Powerful Presentations   22

3

Write for Results   54

4

Supervise Assertively   **71**

5

Create Quality

89

6

Run Effective Meetings

105

7

Manage Conflict Productively   **120**

8

Negotiate to Win   136

9

Conduct Successful Interviews   147

10
Develop Your Organization   *165*

11
Plan and Problem Solve   *191*

12

Find More Time in Your Day   **204**

13

Achieve Personal Success   **214**

14

Manage Your Boss   231

ACKNOWLEDGMENTS

The success of any writing project often depends on the efforts of many people whose names never appear on the cover, and this book is no exception. Specifically we'd like to thank:

Millie Myers for constructing checklists 27–29, 31, and 34, and for editing the first version of this book.

Ted Cook for creating the first drafts of checklists 50, 112, 114, and 116.

The thousands of managers we've worked with whose needs and questions served as the impetus for the book and for the lists themselves.

The researchers and theoreticians who provided the underpinnings for our checklists.

And we are especially grateful to our families. Their contributions to *Smart Moves* are far greater than they know. Di, Suzy, and our children believed in us, supported us, prodded us, and, most important, love us.

PREFACE

We are all managers, regardless of title, rank, profession, or the size or function of the organizations that employ us. We all manage ourselves and our own tasks, we all manage other people (officially or not), and we can all improve our effectiveness by managing *smarter*.

That is one of the most important lessons our combined sixty years of experience as management teachers, consultants, and trainers have taught us.

Another important lesson is that the techniques and principles that enable us to manage smarter are based on looking forward to events rather than reacting to them. The truly successful manager anticipates problems and prevents their occurrence. He or she foresees opportunities and takes advantage of them.

Finally, we've learned that management theory is fine so long as it can ultimately help us solve practical problems. The easiest advice to follow is direct, concise, and jargon-free.

These are the useful lessons we've incorporated into this book. *Smart Moves* provides over 1,600 tips, steps, facts, and strategies that will help you in any management situation. This book presents practical advice based on sound theories of psychology, communication, and management, but it breaks free of those theories. The tools offered to you here are grounded in volumes of research. We've studied the research and synthesized it so that you won't have to. We've presented it in the form of checklists to provide you with a minimum of theory and a maximum of immediate applications.

The ideas in this book cut across job titles, types of organizations, and functional specialties. No matter what you do or for whom you do it, you must communicate, plan, solve problems, interview people, manage time, work with groups, negotiate disagreements, create quality, manage yourself, and manage others.

Following the advice of this book, you will be able to control your organizational environment more successfully. It is written so you will pass each management test the first time you take it, even if you don't have previous experience to profit from. Each checklist that you master teaches you one more smart move.

We developed this checklist approach first for a small book called *The Manager's Book of Lists*, which we published in 1988. We then revised and expanded that book to create the first edition of *Smart Moves*, adding many new checklists, four new chapters, and the *Action Index*. That index, in the back of the book, gives you immediate reference to the checklists that will help you solve forty of the most perplexing management problems around.

The response to the publication of *Smart Moves* in 1990 was tremendously gratifying. More than 40,000 copies were sold in that first year alone, the book appeared on lists of business best-sellers, and our publisher eventually went through twelve printings. A dozen editions were published around the world, from France to Indonesia, South Korea to Germany. Feedback from our readers and clients has led us to write several more books together, including the sequel *Smart Moves for People in Charge*. And now we have brought *Smart Moves* up to date, revising many of the checklists and commentary and looking ahead to a new century of management challenges.

FOUR WAYS TO USE THIS BOOK

1. Read *Smart Moves* from cover to cover as you would any self-improvement text. Use a marker to highlight those ideas you find especially promising in light of your goals. You may even wish to record the most relevant ones on an index card that can double as your page marker.

2. As you have time, while waiting for a meeting to start or when stuck in traffic, skim the pages to revisit lists that you feel you will be able to use the most. Study them until their prescriptions become so familiar that you'll be certain to apply them appropriately as the need arises.

3. This book will benefit you the most whenever you face a particularly challenging management situation. Immediately consult the Action Index for instant reference to the checklists that will help you to meet that challenge. We have also provided notations within lists to help you locate the other lists that may help you in a given situation. You'll find these cross-references in parentheses.

4. Be sure to make a permanent place for *Smart Moves* on your desk or in your briefcase. When challenges arise, you'll never want it to be as far away as your bookshelf.

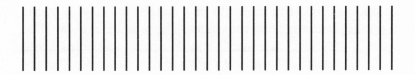

1. Communicate Successfully

THE MOVIE *Cool Hand Luke* provides us with what has become a memorable if not a classic scene. Luke, played by Paul Newman, has just been returned to the labor camp after another unsuccessful attempt to escape. The warden, played by Strother Martin, stands at the top of his porch stairs, glares at Luke handcuffed and kneeling on the ground, and drawls, "What we have here is a failure to communicate."

Every day in this country managers prove that "a failure to communicate" occurs not only in labor camps but anyplace where people come together for productive purposes. Some management researchers have even concluded that communication failures represent the single greatest problem for management today.

Two compelling arguments support this conclusion. The first is that the variety and complexity of a manager's audience has drastically increased over the last few years. Whether communicating up, down, sideways, or outside the organization, managers are finding that the receivers of their messages are more diverse, more sophisticated, and more demanding. The memos, briefings, speeches, and pep talks that worked in the past may not be successful today.

The second reason is that communication is the most common activity of any manager. A number of studies point out that the majority of a manager's day is spent sending and receiving messages. These studies show that about 75% of a manager's day is spent communicating with others. That's right. If you were to construct a diary of your typical workday, you'd find that three-fourths of your time is spent listening, talking, reading, or writing—communicating. Is it any wonder that "a failure to communicate" has been diagnosed as the plague of modern management?

Yet some managers have found an antidote for this affliction. These managers stand out as excellent communicators. They achieve their intended results whenever they talk or write, regardless of the audience. And their listening skills keep them constantly in touch with bosses, team members, peers, customers, and others. Invariably they come across as people who mean what they say, say what they mean, and know what others say and mean.

Managers who lack these skills—and who unfortunately represent much of the population in question—look at their more effective colleagues with admiration and wonderment and maybe a touch of jealousy. "How does she do it?" they wonder. "I wish I could communicate as successfully. If only I could use language as well, or read situations as accurately."

The checklists in this section are designed to help make this wish a reality. We've constructed these lists with two basic assumptions. First, successful communicators approach communication in a different frame of mind than do unsuccessful communicators. Successful communicators do more than simply transmit written or spoken messages. They recognize that communication is a complex process requiring adaptation to each time, place, and audience. Ineffective communicators, on the other hand, fail to acknowledge the complexity of communication and consequently fail to adapt.

The second assumption of these lists is that excellent

communicators are also excellent listeners. They realize that the only way you can adapt your message to the current situation is to have information relevant to your audience's needs, values, and concerns. And although this information is available to both effective and ineffective communicators, only the effective communicators seek it out. They listen carefully, anticipate sensibly, and read as many nonverbal signals as they can.

So study the lists that follow and practice their advice. If you're determined, you'll escape from the shackles of shoddy communication.

#1

Eight Sensible Assumptions about Communication

1. **Communication skills are acquired more than they are inborn.**
   You were born crying, not speaking. You learned how to speak by imitating others—that learning need never end.
2. **Assume the next message you send will be misunderstood.**
   You will thus communicate more thoughtfully, look for feedback, and examine yourself first whenever you don't get your desired results.
3. **Don't worry about being clear; worry about being understood.**
   Ask yourself, "How can I send this message in such a way that I will not be misunderstood?" (3)
4. **The meaning of a word cannot be found in a dictionary.**
   Definitions are in dictionaries; meanings are in people. We don't transmit meaning; we transmit mes-

sages (words and behaviors) that represent and elicit meaning in our listeners' minds.

5. **The meaning people get from you comes less from what you say than from how you say it.**
   In fact, your tone of voice and your body language (your *nonverbal* communication) account for over 90% of the meaning received.

6. **Whenever two people are in each other's presence, they communicate.**
   Even when you don't think you're sending messages, you are. They may not be the messages you want to send, but the other person is receiving them. "You cannot *not* communicate." (8)

7. **87% of the information stored in people's minds entered through their eyes.**
   When your words conflict with your actions, your listener will believe the actions.

8. **Communication is a complex, ongoing, dynamic, and changing process.**
   It is not the simple exchange of words that most people think it is. More can go wrong than go right. And it falls apart if you don't keep fixing it.

#2
Six Ways to Learn More about Yourself as a Communicator

1. **Ask for feedback.**
   There are probably several people close enough to you to observe your communications regularly. Ask these people how well they think you are doing. Chances are they have stored up several observations they will share for the asking. Be specific with your requests so they will be the same with their feedback. Don't be defensive when you hear it. (138)

2. Look for feedback.

If you are a highly observant person who cares about your impact on others, you will rarely have to ask for feedback from others. You'll know how you're coming off to other people from their verbal and especially their nonverbal reactions to you. Too many of us are afraid to acknowledge such feedback, for fear of what we'll see.

3. Tape-record your voice.

This is a good way to check the pronunciation, speed, tone, and vocal variation of your speech. Experiment with your voice to achieve new effects. Be prepared, however, for almost certain dissatisfaction when you first hear your voice played back on a tape recorder.

4. Record yourself on videotape.

Almost as great as the fear of speaking in public is the fear of *seeing* yourself speak in public. Not many people are interested in seeing themselves on videotape, probably because the exercise is so eye opening. You'll see mannerisms and hear speech patterns you never knew you had.

5. Look in a mirror.

Check out your total body image in a full length mirror. Look at the impact of your clothing, the length and style of your hair, the way you hold your body, the overall expression on your face, and so on. Is this the body image you want to send? (127)

6. Listen to yourself.

Most of us need to record our voice in order to hear it because we're so busy thinking about what we're going to say next while we speak that we never really hear our own words. Every once in a while, make yourself aware of your voice. Suspend your thinking and slow down long enough to hear how you sound to other people, and to give yourself the opportunity to weed out undesirable words and sounds.

#3

Eight Strategies for Getting People to Listen to You

1. **Picture your goal in communicating.**
   Know exactly what response you want from your listener. Before you speak, visualize what you want the listener to look like, feel like, and do as a result of your words. In other words, how do you intend to change the listener?

2. **Know your listeners.**
   Who are they? What do they already know? How much detail do they need? What have they experienced prior to your message? How do they feel? What do they want to hear? Are they paying attention? Do they care about you and what you have to say? (12)

3. **Know yourself as a communicator.**
   Every human being has a unique way of sending messages. What is your individual style? How do your values, thought patterns, vocabulary, tone of voice, speech habits, moods, body language, and overall presence affect the meaning listeners receive? (2, 28)

4. **Put your listeners in the picture.**
   Use vivid language, tell complete stories, and paint full pictures that listeners can "see" with their ears. Use examples, metaphors, and analogies. Use fewer words and steer clear of euphemistic language. Choose words that convey specific, concrete images. (29)

5. **Convince your listeners.**
   Show your conviction, confidence, and enthusiasm through tone of voice and body language. Don't overqualify, excessively preface, or apologize for messages as you send them. Shun exaggeration and overstatement. Appeal to the self-interest of your listeners, who continually ask, "What's in it for me?" (29)

6. **Stroke your listeners.**
   Leave your listeners feeling good about themselves and about you. Be supportive and caring. Don't accuse, belittle, violate expectations, or overgeneralize. Be a good listener to your listeners. Use their names in your message. Make them glad they listened to you.
7. **Control time and place.**
   Send messages when listeners are ready for them and feel the need for them—not when *you* want to send them. Choose a location that is consistent with and reinforces the meaning you wish to convey.
8. **Assess and respond to results.**
   What are your listeners telling you? What did they do as a result of your message? Have you been understood? Why or why not? What will you do differently next time?

#4

Eleven Advantages of Listening

1. **Keeps you out of trouble.**
   A good listener heeds instructions, suggestions, and warnings. People rarely have cause to get upset at someone who pays attention to them.
2. **Tells you what's going on.**
   Life is a total learning experience. Things are happening around you all the time. The more you hear and understand those things, the more you learn personally and professionally from your experience.
3. **Makes you more competent.**
   The more information you have about your job, the more successfully you will perform it. Listening is the way to get more knowledge than most others have.
4. **Makes you look intelligent.**
   That's right! Not only does listening increase your intelligence, it makes you *look* intelligent. Consider the

qualities you attribute to a person of few words. Stupidity is probably not one of them.

5. **Increases your power.**
   "Knowledge is power," the saying goes. The power of knowledge gained through listening is that you have more data at your disposal than others. Your actions are well informed and appropriate.

6. **Helps you understand others.**
   Is there anything more important than understanding the needs, motivations, and values of those around you? It is essential to know what it takes to get a subordinate or a superior to respond as you desire. What better way is there to learn what makes other people tick than to listen to them?

7. **Wins respect.**
   How often have you heard another person say, ". . . at least he listened to me"? Couldn't you feel the respect that had been earned by the person who really listened?

8. **Negotiates for you.**
   The two keys to getting what you want from others are knowing what they're willing to give and what it will take to get them to give more. The only way to learn these is to listen, listen, listen. (81–86)

9. **Defuses anger in others.**
   The best initial response to emotion is made with your ears. When we listen to an angry person, we come to understand the cause of the anger, we demonstrate our empathy, and we allow the venting that will ultimately make the person more rational. It is folly to attempt to reason with anger before we can understand it, empathize with it, and defuse it. (76)

10. **Builds self-esteem in others.**
    When you stop what you're doing to listen to someone, you are saying, "I value you and what you have to

say." This is one of the surest ways to build self-esteem in subordinates, children, your spouse, and just about anyone else in your life. (102)

11. **Brings love into your life.**
The most convincing expression of love and caring is to give the gift of listening. After all, who stops to listen to people they don't like? Furthermore, one of the quickest ways to get people to think highly of you, if not love you, is to listen to them. Notice how children judge parental love by whether father and mother show an interest in them through listening.

#5

Twelve Techniques to Improve Your Listening

1. **Shut up.**
You can't talk and listen at the same time.

2. **Recognize that listening is something you do for personal success.**
You don't listen just to be nice to others. Listening earns power, respect, and love and gets you the information you need to be effective. (4)

3. ***Want* to listen better.**
View listening as a small investment of time and energy that produces an enormous return in understanding.

4. **Become less self-centered.**
You're about the only one who believes that you and what you have to say are more important than the other person and what he or she has to say. Maybe you're wrong.

5. **Prepare to listen.**
Think about the speaker and the topic in advance when possible. Set goals for what you hope to learn.

6. **Work hard at listening.**

   Most people speak at an average rate of 120 words per minute. The average listening capacity is about 480 words per minute, or four times faster. This differential causes our minds to wander when another person is speaking. If we can give our speaker a little more concentration—say about 200 wpm of our listening capacity—our minds won't wander. We achieve this by making eye contact, by thinking intently about what is being said, by standing or sitting upright, and by asking questions.

7. **Check for nonverbal cues.**

   Look for what the speaker may be telling you through body language. Listen for tone of voice. (8)

8. **Hold your fire.**

   Don't interrupt. Suspend judgments while the person is talking. Pretend that *everything* she is saying is valid (it *is*, in the sense that she believes it) at least until she stops talking. If you begin to get angry, stop the person, talk about your anger, then have her proceed.

9. **Don't plan your response while the person is talking.**

   You need only a few seconds to think about your response before giving it. The other person will wait for you. There's nothing wrong with a little silence between that person's words and yours.

10. **Overcome distractions.**

    Ignore noisy surroundings. Fight distractions in the situation or in the speaker.

11. **When you need to hear *everything* a person is saying, say to yourself, "Right now, understanding this person's feelings is the most important thing in my life."**

    This is the time to focus *all* of your 480 wpm listening capacity on the speaker. You'll know you've done your job if you are exhausted afterward.

12. **Practice making the decisions you need to make about people and events without coming to final conclusions about them.**

Once you have decided what is true or right you spend your energy defending your conclusion, and you're not likely to listen to disagreement with it. It is better to *act*, when you must, while keeping open the possibility that later you might change your mind.

#6

Ten Types of Words to Use Carefully

1. Jargon.

The technical language of your profession is confusing to those who don't use it every day. Using jargon also alienates listeners who judge you as inconsiderate for not knowing it troubles them.

2. Euphemisms.

Confusion may result from glossing over negative concepts, e.g., referring to taxation as "revenue enhancement." But perhaps the greatest damage done by euphemistic language is that it weakens the images provided to listeners: "sweat" is a strong word, but "perspiration" is weak.

3. Idioms.

The language peculiar to a people or community can be colorful, but also confusing to outsiders ("The car needs washed" is popular in western Pennsylvania). When used among some listeners, your childhood or regional idioms can lower their opinion of you.

4. Slang.

If a word is not in the dictionary, be careful using it—especially when it is important to make a positive impression.

5. **Profanity.**
   The impact you may gain with an off-color remark can be more than offset by the offense taken, but not always acknowledged, by your listeners.

6. **Office- or Company-Specific Phrases.**
   Keep your office terms where they serve a useful purpose—in your office. Referring to a particular personnel document as "HRD-9" in front of outsiders is clear evidence of insensitivity.

7. **Red Flag Words.**
   Words that elicit a strong emotional reaction—e.g., referring to a woman as a "girl"—offend people. They will stop listening and focus on that word.

8. **Vague or Abstract Language.**
   What does it mean when you tell someone, "Please do it as soon as you can"? Provide clarity, specificity, and concreteness. Leave no doubt in the meaning of your words.

9. **Overly Complex Words.**
   Don't make the mistake of believing that $50 words are better than $5 words. More pompous they are, more communicative they aren't. In other words, we wish to proscribe the superfluous display of one's vocabulary.

10. **Clichés.**
    Using phrases that people consider to be trite or hackneyed causes *you* to appear trite or hackneyed. Avoid worn-out expressions like "You can't tell a book. . ." and "You can lead a horse to water. . ."

#7

Twenty-eight Terms All Managers Should Know

1. **Benchmarking.**
   Comparing the practices within your company to the

best practices in some of the most successful companies inside or outside your industry.

2. **Bottom Line.**

   Taken from the bottommost figure on a profit-and-loss statement. It refers to the most important measure of success in a particular organization: profit, service, productivity, expense reduction, or some other.

3. **Break-even Point.**

   The dollar value where profits begin. The point where revenues equal costs.

4. **Cash Cow.**

   Any product or service that is highly profitable.

5. **Centralization.**

   Maintaining power and decision making at headquarters or at the top of the organization. The opposite is *decentralization*—pushing decision making and power downward and outward.

6. **DIRFT.**

   "Do it right the first time." The most basic philosophy of quality improvement. (48, 49)

7. **80-20 Rule (Pareto's Law).**

   The majority of your productivity is accounted for by a minority of your activity. For example, 80% of your sales probably come from 20% of your customers.

8. **Fixed Costs.**

   Costs incurred by an organization regardless of the number of products produced.

9. **Halo Effect.**

   Tendency to evaluate a person's overall qualifications or performance on the basis of a specific trait or accomplishment.

10. **JIT (Just in Time).**

    An inventory system based on the Japanese model of minimizing inventory-control costs. Supplies arrive just before they are needed.

11. Learning Curve.

The longer you do something the more proficient you become.

12. Line vs. Staff.

Anyone directly responsible for producing the product or service is in a *line* position; anyone who provides support is in a *staff* position (e.g., the Personnel Department).

13. Liquidity Ratio.

$$\frac{\text{Current Assets}}{\text{Current Liabilities}}$$

14. Marketing Mix.

Combination of four P's (Price, Place, Product, Promotion) designed to satisfy customer needs.

15. MBO (Management by Objectives).

A management philosophy based on the principle that performance should be measured by quantifiable objectives. It suggests managers evaluate employees based more on their results than on how they achieve those results.

16. MBWA (Managing by Wandering Around).

A philosophy that argues for getting out of your office and talking to the people on the line.

17. MIS (Management Information System).

Any system that links decision makers with information—usually incorporating computers.

18. Open-Door Policy.

A policy allowing employees access to their supervisor at any time without necessarily making an appointment.

19. Product Life Cycle.

The theory that all products and services progress through four stages: introduction, growth, maturity, and decline.

20. Pygmalion Effect.

High expectations for another's performance tend to

result in high performance; low expectations result in low performance.

21. **Quality Improvement Team.**

A small group of employees in a department who meet voluntarily and with support from management to generate ideas to enhance productivity and improve quality. They present ideas to management for approval and often monitor the implementation of approved projects. (57)

22. **QWL (Quality of Work Life).**

A belief in the importance of enriching the intrinsic motivating factors on the job, including such factors as safety and health, challenge, involvement, and significance.

23. **Re-engineering.**

Process of designing organization so that employees focus on processes (what they do to serve the customers) rather than function (job titles, hierarchy, and duties).

24. **ROE (Return on Equity).**

$$\frac{\text{Profits}}{\text{Investments}}$$

25. **Span of Control.**

The number of people reporting to a given supervisor or manager.

26. **Stakeholder.**

Anyone who has a vested interest in your company (A stockholder has strictly a financial interest).

27. **TQM (Total Quality Management).**

Comprehensive approach to product or service improvement. TQM is driven by a belief that there is always opportunity for improvement in products and processes of an organization.

28. **Variable Costs.**

Expenses that fluctuate depending on the number of units produced.

#8

Sixteen Ways We Send Messages Without Words

1. **Eyes.**
   They are the most communicative organs in the body. The eyes tell if someone is happy, sad, interested, intense, surprised, lying, sick, or in a dozen other conditions. And the sender has very little control over what the eyes say.

2. **Face.**
   The mouth can scowl, grimace, pout, smile, or communicate pomposity. Flushed cheeks may reveal discomfort, embarrassment, or a lack of physical stamina. A raised eyebrow can quiet a screaming child.

3. **Hair.**
   Some people make judgments of others based upon the color of their hair, and whether the color, or the hair, appears to be natural. The amount of hair a man has remaining on his head may speak to some, as well as whether he maintains a moustache or beard—and how well. Hair style is often an indicator of a person's values, religious beliefs, or socioeconomic status.

4. **Body.**
   Our society draws profound (and not always consistent) inferences about people according to whether they are tall, short, fat, or thin.

5. **Posture.**
   Leaning, kneeling, slouching, slumping, and standing erect all create distinct images in others' minds.

6. **Gestures.**
   Hand movements either reinforce or contradict what is said, and can even serve as effective substitutes for words.

7. **Clothing.**

   Whole books have been written about how clothes "shout," especially in professional settings. (127)

8. **Cosmetics.**

   Well-applied makeup can create a positive impression; sloppy or excessive cosmetics send unfavorable messages. Perfumes and colognes have the same power.

9. **Accessories.**

   We draw inferences about people from the things they carry around with them—the look of their purses or wallets, the presence and quality of briefcases, the newspapers tucked under their arms, whether they are holding umbrellas, and so on.

10. **Voice.**

    "Vocalic" messages include tone, pitch, emphasis, inflection, rate, volume, vocabulary, pronunciation, dialect, and fluency. Studies have shown these factors to be as much as five times more potent than the actual words uttered. (17)

11. **Touch.**

    Despite recently developed taboos on touch in the workplace, service workers, especially in the health professions, are being taught how to use touch to improve their rapport with clients. The most important touch message is the handshake—doesn't it tell you a lot about the other person?

12. **Behavior.**

    The Book of Ecclesiasticus says, "Words show the wit of man, but actions his meaning." People constantly observe your behavior to deduce what they consider to be the truth behind your words.

13. **Surroundings.**

    Messages exist in the places you live and work. For example, what does your office say about you? Does its size and location speak of your importance in the company? Is your desk messy? Where are your side chairs located? Are family pictures present? What do your furniture, books, and graffiti say about you?

14. **Personal space.**

Personal space is the distance you maintain between yourself and others when you speak to them, and whether you violate what they establish as *their* personal space. These distances vary across cultures. Two Arabs are likely to stand closer to each other in conversation than two Americans.

15. **Place.**

Choose locations for your conversations that will reinforce, not detract from, the meaning you want the listener to receive.

16. **Time.**

What does your use of time say to others? Do you keep people waiting and get to meetings late? Do you fail to meet agreed-upon deadlines?

#9

Fifteen Ideas for Better Use of Your Telephone

1. **Make appointments for the date and time of your call.**

This increases the probability the person you're calling will answer. (120)

2. **Before calling, outline the topics to discuss and the specific outcomes you desire.**

Keep the discussion focused on these topics.

3. **Before dialing, picture the other person.**

Anticipate the likely reaction to what you have to say, given your knowledge of the listener. (12)

4. **Be kind to phone answerers.**

If you fail to reach the person you're calling, don't be

gruff or otherwise indicate displeasure. Don't object to being put on hold. You may need a favor someday from the screener who is trying to help you.

5. **Leave messages that get results.**

   Give the screener something to motivate your target to return the call. Instead of saying, "Tell him I called," try, "I've lined up that contact he asked for." When you cannot honestly make your call sound that important, put humor in your message. If it solicits a chuckle from the target, a return call is likely to follow.

6. **When the other person answers your call, ask whether he or she has time to speak.**

   One good question is, "Is this a good time for me to call?" Don't ever say, "Are you busy?"

7. **Consider answering your own telephone and placing your own calls.**

   You will add a personal touch to your conversations.

8. **Don't allow your telephone screener to ask, "May I tell Miss Meyers what your call is in regard to?"**

   This is unnerving to many callers. They may not want to share their message with the screener, or may want you to hear everything from them.

9. **Make a special effort to use vivid language, detailed stories, and full explanations on the telephone.**

   This compensates for the absence of nonverbal cues in your messages.

10. **Avoid doing something else while talking.**

    Typing, writing, reading, or doodling during the conversation may disturb the other person, who is almost certain to hear your lack of involvement in your tone of voice.

11. **Whenever your message contains complex, detailed, or critical information, communicate in person or in writing.**

When you can't see the listener, you don't know how much effort that person is making to understand you. Quantitative information is more effectively transmitted on paper, on a computer monitor screen, or via facsimile transmission.

12. **Follow up important phone conversations with a confirming memo.**

You may need the documentation later, and it will pinpoint misunderstandings.

13. **Once you achieve your objectives, end the conversation.**

Disengage from chatty callers by telling them you have a pressing deadline, by hanging up while you have the initiative in the conversation, by feigning an incoming long distance call on your other line, or with another strategy that works for you.

14. **Make a record of important telephone calls.**

Note action agreed to or any need for follow-up.

15. **Evaluate the impact on your business before installing an automated telephone system.**

Customers and other callers may be put off when their call is answered by a recorded message. Most automated systems are a convenience for the company but an inconvenience for the customer.

#10

Sixteen Questions to Ask about Your Communication Style

You should be able to answer "yes" to all of these questions.

1. When you have something to say, are you open and honest about your need to say it?
2. Are you aware when you communicate that the words

you choose may not mean the same thing to other people that they do to you? (1)

3. Do you recognize that the message you receive may not be the same one the other person intended to send?

4. Before communicating, do you ask yourself questions about who your receiver is and how that will affect his or her reception of your message? (12)

5. As you speak face-to-face with someone, do you watch for indications that you are understood? (8)

6. Do you make messages as brief and to the point as possible?

7. Do you avoid the use of jargon with those who may not understand it? (6)

8. Do you avoid slang, idioms, and colloquialisms with those who may be put off by them or not understand them? (6)

9. Do you try not to use words that may upset or distract the receiver of your message? (6)

10. Do you recognize that how you say something is just as important as what you say? (8)

11. Do you recognize the nonverbal messages you send and how well they conform to the meaning you want to get across? (8)

12. Do you carefully consider whether your message would be best understood by the receiver in a face-to-face meeting, over the telephone, or in writing?

13. Do you form opinions about what others say based on what you *hear* them say, and not on what you think of them as people? (5)

14. Do you make a genuine effort to listen to ideas with which you don't agree?

15. Do you look for ways to improve your listening skills? (5)

16. Are you using e-mail as efficiently and as effectively as you can?

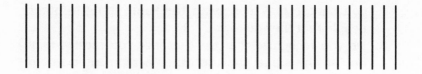

2. Deliver Powerful Presentations

WE'VE BEEN college teachers, trainers, and consultants for sixty years, combined. We've shared countless ideas with thousands of people, who have also taught us many things. One of the most important and recurring lessons we've learned is that the fear of public speaking transcends intellect, age, socioeconomic class, occupation, industry, and hierarchical rank. It even affects college teachers, trainers, and consultants.

Competent professionals, secure in their abilities to manage human, financial, and physical resources, can be transformed into quivering masses of anxiety when called upon to "say a few words." It's almost as if managers develop split personalities. One persona, reflecting control, security, and competence, is exhibited in the day-to-day conduct of business. The other persona, full of fear, insecurity, and doubt, comes alive any time the manager must give a formal presentation.

What is it about a podium that can transform an otherwise confident professional with an engaging personality into a terrified amateur who appears to have only recently recovered from a frontal lobotomy? How can a highly paid manager who feels totally secure planning a million-dollar budget become tongue-tied when presenting that budget to a group of higher-ups?

The answer to both of these questions can be summarized simply: we fear things we either don't understand or don't have experience with. And since our formal education system generally shortchanges us in the teaching of communication skills, few managers enter their profession with a practiced knowledge of public speaking.

Just as our consulting teaches us that fear of public speaking is rampant in corporate America, it also teaches us that knowledge, practice, and one or two positive experiences will alleviate the fear. That's right. You can *learn* to speak with clarity, control, and impact. We've seen dozens of managers undergo significant and dramatic changes in their public speaking skills. Competency previously manifested only away from the podium was brought to the podium. And all they had to do was understand how to give a speech and get a few positive experiences "under their belts."

The checklists in this section are designed to help you understand how to give a speech. From the initial stages of deciding what to say to the final stage of conducting a question-and-answer session, these lists provide practical, tested advice.

When you're finished studying and applying the advice contained in these checklists, you'll realize that speakers are not born, they are made. You will also realize that the supposed "gifts" which some speakers manifest with apparent ease can be acquired by anyone.

Once you arrive at these realizations you'll notice a dramatic change in your attitude toward public speaking. It will no longer be something to be feared and avoided, but rather an opportunity to be prized and sought. You will realize, just as others have, that the podium provides the quickest route to the executive suite.

#11

Eleven Steps for Constructing a Speech

1. **Determine how you intend to change the audience.**
   This is your speech's purpose. Create it by completing this sentence: "When my speech is ended, the audience will. . . ."

2. **What do you know about the audience?**
   How will you take advantage of audience factors in your favor, and how will you overcome those operating to your disadvantage? (12)

3. **Brainstorm all the ideas central to your speech purpose and the major points you want to make.**
   Don't worry yet about their order or about relationships among them; just write these ideas down as you think of them. A good way to do this is to create a "cognitive map." Write your speech purpose in the center of a large sheet of paper. Then write central ideas as you think of them on rays emanating out of the center in all directions.

4. **Look for natural clusters among the ideas coming out of your speech purpose.**
   Which ideas, or clusters of ideas, represent *main* points? Draw connecting lines to show clusters. A good speech contains from three to five main points. If you have more, you either have too much to say or you haven't done enough clustering. Which items represent *supporting* points? Draw dotted lines from them to the main points they support.

5. **Do your clusters suggest the best structure for the speech?**
   See "Seven Strategies for Organizing Your Speech." (13)

6. **Write the outline of your speech.**
   Now you're ready to convert your map into the linear

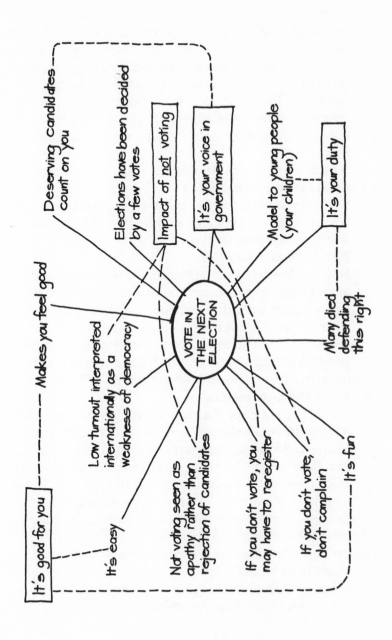

VOTE IN THE NEXT ELECTION

Deserving candidates count on you

Elections have been decided by a few votes

Impact of not voting

It's your voice in government

Model to young people (your children)

It's your duty

Makes you feel good

Many died defending this right

Low turnout interpreted internationally as a weakness of democracy

It's good for you

It's easy

Not voting seen as apathy rather than rejection of candidates

If you don't vote, you may have to reregister

If you don't vote, don't complain

It's fun

outline that will serve as your notes. Transfer the central ideas and supporting points from the map onto your note cards in outline form. Arrange your ideas onto three levels. Assign Roman numerals to your three to five central ideas. Each central idea may have anywhere from one to five supporting ideas, which may each have more ideas in support of them. Flesh out your notes with additional points as you think of them.

7. **Which of your points can be enhanced or simplified through visual aids?**

   What are the images you most want them to remember? Create these images and plan the points at which they will be shown. (23)

8. **Write the introduction.**

   How will you get their attention? How will you generate interest in your topic? What will you do to establish rapport with the audience? How will you earn their respect? What tone do you want to set? What do you want to tell them up front about your speech purpose? Within 20 seconds you'll have to answer their question: "Why should I listen to you?" (20)

9. **Write the conclusion.**

   Go back to your speech purpose; the change you want in your audience should be reinforced in your closing. Relate your closing to your opening. Throw the ball into their court. Tell them what you want them to do. Take them into the future. Build to a climax. Raise your level of intensity to what it was during the introduction. (Some speakers advocate writing the conclusion before doing anything else.)

10. **Prepare for the question-and-answer period, if there is to be one.**

    Review "Twelve Techniques for Conducting a Successful Question-and-Answer Session." (24)

Vote in the next election

I. It's good for you
    A. It's easy
        1. usually takes fifteen minutes
        2. in your own neighborhood
    B. It's fun
    C. It makes you feel good

II. It's your voice in government
    A. Deserving candidates count on you
    B. If you don't vote, don't complain

III. Impact of not voting
    A. Elections are decided by a few votes
        1. Kennedy-Nixon in 1960
    B. It's seen as apathy, not a statement
        1. your vote is the strongest statement
        2. apathy seen internationally as a weakness of our democracy
    C. You may have to register again

IV. It's the thing to do
    A. Your duty as a citizen
    B. Many died to defend your right
        1. it's what's special about our system
        2. many other people never had this right
    C. Be a model for your children

If you're asked to make impromptu remarks and you don't have time to do steps 1–10:

11. **Pose three important questions on your topic and proceed to answer them.**

    These questions substitute for the central ideas of a speech, and they establish your speech purpose, as well. Ask questions beginning with three of these words: who, what, where, when, why, and how. Answer each of the questions in turn. Alternatively, discuss "Three reasons to . . ."; "Three important features of . . ."; "Three steps to . . ."; etc. The more you talk, the further you provide the supporting points necessary to document and elaborate on the three central ideas you selected.

#12
Fifteen Questions to Ask about Your Audience

1. What do they already know about this topic?
2. How do they feel about this topic?
3. What do they know about me?
4. How do they feel about me?
5. Are external circumstances likely to affect the audience's response to my speech?
6. Do they want me to be here?
7. Who are the major opinion leaders in the group?
8. Who is the formal leader? The informal leader?
9. Should my speech attempt to accomplish different purposes with various audience members?
10. Is there an expert on my topic in the group?

11. What are the questions or objections this audience is likely to have?
12. What is the best way to create rapport with them?
13. What do they value?
14. What demographic characteristics of the audience do I need to keep in mind?
15. What strategies have worked well with them in the past?

#13

Seven Strategies for Organizing Your Speech

1. **Chronological.**
   Arrange your ideas in a time sequence. "In the past we did A, now we do B, but soon we'll be able to do C."
2. **Topical.**
   Organize your ideas according to the major logical subdivisions in your speech purpose. *Who, what, where, when, how,* and *why* represent a simple, logical, topical pattern.
3. **Spatial.**
   Use this structure to explain ideas whose location is of primary interest. "The three possible sites for our new branch are. . . ."
4. **Problem-Solution.**
   Define the nature of the problem, identify its causes, and then propose a solution.
5. **Cause-Effect.**
   Elaborate on the causes of a given condition or situation and describe its major effects or consequences.
6. **Cost-Benefit.**
   Contrast the major costs (or weaknesses) of a proposal or program with its benefits or strengths.

7. **Need-Fulfillment.**
   Describe a need of your audience and then proceed to tell them how they can fulfill it.

#14
Eight Ways to Create Appealing Speech Titles

1. **Convey the major benefit of listening to your speech.**
   The title "PowerTalk: How to Get People to Listen to You" says more than "Effective Communication Skills." "How to . . ." titles tell people what they can expect to get out of your talk.

2. **Use numbers to raise curiosity.**
   "The Four Secrets of Leadership" is a more intriguing title than simply "The Secrets of Leadership."

3. **Use subtitles and tag lines for greater impact.**
   Notice how "Criticism and Praise: Giving It and Getting It" is made more powerful by the explanation of the main title.

4. **Lengthen titles to enrich the look of your talk.**
   The title "Your Important Relationships" can be profitably lengthened to "Putting More Into and Getting More Out of the Relationships Important to You."

5. **Create intrigue.**
   Another strategy is to keep your potential audience guessing about the thrust of your presentation. Consider "Ten Things Your Attorney, Banker, and Accountant Never Told You About Running a Business." Will you learn what these advisors *should* have told you or something their expertise doesn't even cover?

6. **Borrow a phrase from your speech.**
   You may have a particularly eloquent or important phrase in your speech that will serve well as a title. Martin Luther King, Jr. did not originally entitle his

stirring speech on the steps of the Lincoln Memorial "I Have a Dream," but we wouldn't call it anything else today.

7. **Ask a question.**

Questions are difficult to brush aside. Change your declarative title into a question, and almost everyone who sees it will try to think of an answer and thereby be hooked by the thesis of your speech. "The War on Drugs" can become "Who's Winning the War on Drugs?"

8. **Use powerful words.**

Some words are especially attention-getting and appealing in titles: *you, how, new, who, free, now, suddenly, amazing, miracle, power, secret, remarkable, startling, magic, challenge.*

#15
Eight Tips for Giving a Good Introduction to a Speaker

1. **Ask for a biography rather than a résumé.**

Distilling someone's résumé into a good introduction is a difficult assignment. Furthermore, you're not likely to please the speaker with what you choose to say about him or her. Instead ask for a three-paragraph biographical description that says what this person would like you to say. Get permission to make minor additions and deletions.

2. **Interview the speaker.**

The very best introductions given on our behalf have been made by people who called us up to interview us before our speech. Some of the best questions we've been asked are "In one sentence, what is your philosophy of . . .?"; "What event in your life has had the most profound impact on your career?"; "What single person has had the most profound impact on your life?"; "What lifelong ambition have you yet to achieve?"

3. **Answer the question, "Why _this_ speaker?"**

   Don't fill the audience's brains with the speaker's credentials, titles, degrees, and awards. They want to know why this particular speaker is standing in front of them. What expertise does she have in _this_ field? Why is he uniquely qualified to be here?

4. **Be upbeat!**

   Sound as though you're excited about this person's presence and as though you can't wait to hear the talk yourself. Unless you're introducing a eulogy, smile and be animated.

5. **Share something of the _person_.**

   Your speaker needs to build instant rapport with the audience. You can help by showing the speaker as a living, breathing, compassionate, and even vulnerable person. But be careful not to embarrass or offend the speaker. Check out your personal touch with the speaker before you speak.

6. **Don't steal the speaker's thunder.**

   Your job is to introduce the speaker, not the topic. The _speaker_ introduces the topic. Find out if there is anything the speaker wants you to divulge beyond the title of the talk. The worst introduction ever given for one of us violated this principle so blatantly that the entire speech was compromised.

7. **Don't say, "Our speaker needs no introduction."**

   How trite! If this is really true, then sit down and shut up.

8. **Say the speaker's name before you say anything else.**

   This isn't a hard and fast rule, but just about every good introduction we've heard opened with the speaker's name. After stating the speaker's name loudly and distinctly, the rest of the introduction seems to flow naturally and effortlessly.

#16

Eighteen Ways to Gain Confidence as a Public Speaker

1. **Adopt a new set of attitudes about your fears.**
   Namely, audiences are rarely hostile; you don't have to be a silver-tongued orator to succeed; you rarely look as nervous as you feel; and a little adrenaline is a good thing to take to the lectern. *Accept* podium anxiety as something that even the most professional speakers experience.

2. **Analyze your audience.**
   The more you know about your audience, the more confident you'll feel. (12)

3. **Prepare, prepare, prepare!**
   The better you know your topic, the more you will feel master of both it and your audience.

4. **Develop reassuring notes.**
   Use a format comfortable for you. Note down your "choreography" to remind yourself when to pause, when to emphasize a point, when to refer to audiovisual aids, and so on. (18)

5. **Imagine being a hit.**
   Beginning two weeks before your presentation, take five minutes each night while lying in bed to create images of success in your mind. See the audience hanging on your every word. See the confident smile on your face. Hear yourself speaking with conviction.

6. **Use audiovisuals to take some of the heat off you.**
   When you're highly nervous, it's nice to have those piercing eyes looking in another direction. (23)

7. **Practice, practice, practice!**
   Deliver your speech three or four times before the real thing; do this until you're comfortable with delivery. Don't practice on the day of the speech.

8. **Get familiar with the room and lectern in advance.**
   This is the *best* place to practice delivering your speech.

9. **Relax, rest, and avoid stimulation.**
   Get lots of rest the night before; limit caffeine intake. (80)

10. **Have your introduction and conclusion down pat.**
    Be confident about your opening and closing. (11)

11. **Establish comfortable room temperature, good lighting, and adequate ventilation.**
    A drowsy audience will upset you further.

12. **Dress for success.**
    Wear something you know you look good in. (126, 127)

13. **Expend a burst of energy.**
    Do something strenuous just before stepping to the lectern. Try a brisk walk or a climb of stairs.

14. **Establish eye contact with a few friendly faces.**
    Protect yourself in the warm gaze of people whom you know or who are nonverbally communicating their support of you.

15. **Speak loudly to dissipate anxiety.**
    This helps release bottled up nervousness.

16. **Use natural humor, as opposed to planned jokes that may fail.**
    The easiest subject to get people to laugh at spontaneously is you. If you do plan a joke, be certain it has neither an ethnic nor a sexist basis; better to bore than offend.

17. **Pretend your mistakes don't happen.**
    Don't be rattled by them; most of your audience won't even notice them. Apologies weaken your position.

18. **Don't take yourself too seriously.**
    Naturally you want to do a good job as a speaker, but don't overestimate the importance of your speech in the scheme of things. Your presentation is not the

earthshaking event to others that it is to you. More-
over, if you screw up, your audience won't remember
what you did nearly as long as you will. Learn to laugh
at your blunders.

#17
Eight Strategies for Improving Your Voice

1. **Record your voice on audiotape.**
   Listen to it objectively. Experiment with different
   tone, pitch, emphasis, speed, volume, and enuncia-
   tion. Volume is an especially important variation to
   practice; count from one to five, increasing and de-
   creasing your loudness until you have expanded your
   capacity for variation.
2. **Try to speak at least as fast as 120 words per
   minute.**
   This is the average speaking rate. Ask friends for feedback on your speed.
3. **Articulate distinctly.**
   Say tongue twisters until you master them. Make a
   concerted effort to pronounce the final consonant
   sound in every word.
4. **Emphasize key words and concepts with your
   voice.**
   "Punch out" the important ideas, the ones you want
   your audience to remember.
5. **Use your voice to create contrast.**
   High and low, loud and soft, excited and reserved.
6. **Practice speaking from deep in your diaphragm.**
   Don't talk through your nose. Try to create vibration
   in your vocal chords.
7. **Ask close associates if they notice any annoying
   vocal mannerisms.**
   Listen for them yourself. You'll be surprised what you

can hear in your own voice if you just set your mind to it.

8. **Take care of your voice.**

   A sore or tired voice needs rest, humidification, and no antihistamines. You might also try sipping hot water or chewing raisins. (17)

#18

Eleven Tips for Writing and Reading a Prepared Speech

1. **Write the way you speak, not the way you write.**

2. **Make each paragraph three to five sentences long.**

   It's easy to lose your place when reading longer paragraphs.

3. **Write with active verbs rather than passive verbs.**

   Active verbs ("We *opened* five new stores") are more powerful and direct than passive verbs ("Five new stores *were opened* by us"). (29)

4. **Limit your sentences to no more than twenty words.**

   Longer sentences are more difficult for your audience to follow.

5. **Speak in first and second person rather than third person.**

   Most of your pronouns should be *I, you, we,* and *us. It, they,* and *them* are impersonal and could give your speech the sound of a lecture. However, avoid excessive use of *I* so as not to appear self-centered.

6. **Type the manuscript neatly and clearly.**

   Use a 13 or 14 point sans serif font style such as Arial. Double space the lines. Do not right-justify the text.

7. **Underline any words or phrases that should be emphasized.**

8. **Write the word "PAUSE" in the manuscript at points where a dramatic pause is appropriate.**

9. **Create a large left- or right hand margin.**
   Insert reminders to refer to audiovisuals and other "stage directions" in it.
10. **Practice reading the speech.**
    You want to deliver it with a maximum of eye contact.
11. **Read the way you speak, not the way you read.**

#19

Twelve Checks to Make in the Room Where You'll Speak

1. **Are the chairs arranged so that everyone is comfortably seated and can see you?**
   Move chairs if you need to.
2. **Is smoking to be allowed?**
   If so, are nonsmokers protected?
3. **Are refreshments available only at a specific time?**
   Can you manage to break at that time?
4. **If you are speaking just before lunch, will you have to end exactly on time?**
   Check with your host or the food service people.
5. **Is the lighting sufficient?**
   Rooms are often not bright enough.
6. **Is it too hot or too cold?**
   The temperature should be between 68 and 72 degrees Fahrenheit (about 20 degrees Celsius).
7. **Is there enough fresh air?**
   Poor ventilation and lack of oxygen will cause drowsiness.
8. **Have outside distractions been controlled?**
   Find ways to control noise from a kitchen, a speaker in the next room, paging beepers, outside traffic, etc. Can house phones in the room be disconnected?

9. **If you requested name tags, have they been provided?**
   Are they readable?

10. **Check that all equipment you will use is operable.**
    Are telephone connections made? Is your computer-based projection system working? Are spare projector bulbs handy?

11. **Test the sound system.**
    Is it loud enough and clear enough? Is the microphone you requested on hand? Do you have the phone number of the sound engineer?

12. **Who unlocks and locks the room?**
    If the room is locked when you show up to practice or give your speech, whom should you call?

#20
Ten Powerful Openers

1. **Ask a rhetorical question.**
   "How many of you are fully satisfied with your success at getting people to listen to you?"

2. **Make a strong, surprising, or ironic statement.**
   "Everything you've ever learned about leadership influence is wrong."

3. **Quote a startling statistic.**
   "The number one fear in life is of speaking before a group."

4. **Disclose something about yourself.**
   "This presentation represents six months of my life."

5. **Demonstrate your knowledge of the audience or their experience.**
   "In your business you succeed by being different." (12)

6. **Quote a pithy aphorism that states the thesis of your speech.**
   "Diplomacy is the art of telling someone to go to hell in such a way that they look forward to the trip." (26)

7. **Look at the audience, then look down in silence as though thinking.**

   They'll wonder what you're up to.

8. **Startle the audience with a visual act or with an aural surprise.**

   Use your imagination. We've seen everything from colorful slides to a handstand, and we've heard everything from sudden music to a starter's pistol.

9. **Refer to a current event that has everyone's attention.**

   If you can relate the event to your topic, you'll be off to a great start.

10. **Give your introducer a concise and hard-hitting statement, possibly with humor, to read about you.**

    Don't expect people to extract a good introduction from your résumé. Don't thank the introducer at length or otherwise draw attention back to him or her; go right into your powerful opening statement. (15)

#21
Seven Ways to Give Your Speech More Impact

1. **Use transitions to link your ideas together.**

   Transitions are words, phrases, or sentences that help you move from point to point in your speech. The simplest transition is to *number* your points ("First . . . second . . .") as you state them. Another transitional strategy is a *question* that you pose and answer. You can *repeat* a phrase from a previous sentence and elaborate on it. Certain words also effect transitions, e. g., *besides, furthermore, in the same way, on the other hand, consequently, in fact, meanwhile, to this end.* Vary your choice of transitions. Any of them will become numbing if used repeatedly.

2. **Use repetition to rivet your audience.**

   Repetition can appear at the beginning of successive sentences, as in Martin Luther King's "I Have a Dream" speech. It can be at the end: "When I was a child, I spoke as a child, I understood as a child, I thought as a child." (1 Corinthians)

3. **Use antithesis to create memorable effects.**

   This technique places contrasting ideas within parallel arrangements of words. From John F. Kennedy: "And so, my fellow Americans: ask not what your country can do for you—ask what you can do for your country."

4. **Create attention through alliteration.**

   When two or more successive or nearby words begin with the same letter you have alliteration. Gerald Ford accomplished this when he said, "My record is one of progress, not platitudes; performance, not promises."

5. **Emphasize a point by asking a rhetorical question.**

   In *The Merchant of Venice* Shylock asks six rhetorical questions to win the audience over: "Hath not a Jew eyes? Hath not a Jew hands, organs, dimensions, senses, affections, passions? . . If you prick us, do we not bleed? If you tickle us, do we not laugh? If you poison us, do we not die? And, if you wrong us, shall we not revenge?"

6. **Paint pictures for the audience with analogies, similes, and metaphors.**

   Connect your idea to something they already know: "Think of our clerical staff as the offensive line of a football team; they have to clear the way for the rest of us to do our job. Without them we're dead."

7. **Appeal to the audience through the rule of three.**

   A series of three ideas is almost always more powerful

than two, four, or more. Consider: "Life, liberty, and the pursuit of happiness"; "Duty, honor, country"; "For thine is the kingdom, and the power, and the glory."

#22
Fourteen Ways to Excite Your Audience

1. **Choose a topic that excites you.**
   Modify an assigned topic so that it takes on a twist of interest for you.
2. **Sleep well the night before.**
3. **Don't eat a heavy meal just before you speak.**
4. **Become familiar with the room, the podium, and the audience.**
   You can then totally immerse yourself in your presentation. (12, 19)
5. **Talk to someone before your speech about the excitement you feel for the topic.**
6. **Don't stray below 120 words per minute, except for effect.**
   This is the average speaking rate; the best motivational speakers average closer to 200 wpm. Going below 120 wpm will cause your listeners' minds to wander. (17)
7. **Use your voice for impact.**
   Change volume, speed, pitch, and emphasis to hold interest. Lower your voice to signal your final words. (17)
8. **Know your opening so well that you can look directly at the audience when you deliver it.**
   Say it with conviction and high energy, and grab them with your eyes. (20)

9. **Use a microphone only if necessary.**

   For audiences of fewer than fifty and in rooms with decent acoustics you'll generally do better with your natural voice. It is almost always better to wear or carry a microphone than to stand behind one affixed to a lectern.

10. **Use a microphone properly.**

    Don't touch it once you begin speaking. Don't turn away or step back from it without raising your voice. When you want to rivet your audience with a point, move closer to the microphone and speak in lowered, hushed tones.

11. **Desert the lectern; move into your audience.**

    Once in a while, break the physical barrier (the front row of seats) they feel exists between you and them.

12. **Show your excitement through body movement, gestures, and posture.**

    Talk to individuals, not to the audience.

13. **Smile with your mouth and with your voice.**

14. **Deliver an uplifting message.**

    Even a mundane or worrisome topic can be delivered with enthusiasm and optimism.

#23

Twenty-six Tips for Using Audiovisual Aids

1. **Use your own equipment when you can.**

   Don't rely on other people unless you're sure they'll come through for you. By bringing your own LCD panel, for instance, you know how it works, how well it works, and that it will be there.

2. **When flying, carry your a.v. material with you on board.**

   It's better to lose your clothing.

3. Expect trouble.

Have a back-up activity planned in case the projectionist doesn't show, the film breaks, the spare bulb blows, or the power dies.

4. Don't overload your audience with visual aids.

A good rule of thumb is one visual aid for each key concept.

5. Be certain people throughout the room can see your visuals.

Preview them from the same distance your audience will see them. Be certain they are not blocked by you, the lectern, or anything else.

6. Speak to the audience, not to the visual aid.

You lose the audience when you show them your back.

If you use films or videos:

7. Don't show obviously dated programs.

The audience is likely to be distracted by the length of skirts or the width of ties. If you are planning to show a training film or video, preview it first.

8. Position TV monitors where all can see without any annoying reflections on the screen.

If you use overheads or an LCD panel:

9. Clean the lens and glass—especially underneath—to remove speckles from the projected image.

10. Position the screen so that it is not under a ceiling light.

11. Don't turn off the lights when showing overheads.

People sleep in the dark. Test to see how much lighting you can sustain in the room while still projecting a sharp image on the screen. You may be surprised to discover that in most rooms you won't have to dim the lights at all.

12. **Don't simply put text on overheads.**

    Use enhancements such as graphics, cartoons, and color. Titles and lists are preferable to sentences and paragraphs.

13. **Display numerical data in graphs and lines, not tables.**

    Visual impact should be felt within five seconds. Full comprehension should not require more than 20 seconds.

If you use computers:

14. **Use software tools that best present your message.**

    Don't get carried away with "bells and whistles" and other special effects. Balance the need to inform with the desire to impress or entertain.

15. **Make sure hardware and software are compatible.**

    If you will deliver the presentation from a file transported on a disc, make sure the program used to save the file "speaks" to the program on the computer you will use to retrieve the file.

16. **Access pages off the world-wide Internet or the company's intranet.**

    Tap into useful data bases, graphics, video clips, and audio files.

If you use 35mm slides:

17. **Make a duplicate of your best slide and insert it at the end of the tray to accompany your closing remarks.**

18. **Place an opaque blank at the beginning and end of your tray.**

    This avoids distracting your audience with a blinding flash of light.

If you use flip charts:

19. **Be careful with pointers, especially the retractable type.**

    You are likely to play with them.

20. Write reminder notes lightly in pencil on each page of the charts you will use.

The notes will be visible only to you. They will remind you of what you intend to write in marker on each page. You could give an entire presentation in this way without any visible notes or memory aids.

21. Position your flip chart properly.

Make it as high as possible. Put it close to the audience, not back in a corner. Don't allow it to block other visual aids, such as a screen, you may also be using. Place it so you do not have to constantly cross in front of it to write; right-handers should position their flip chart stage left, and vice versa.

22. Use appropriate flip-chart markers.

Use only wet markers, never dry-erase, on paper. Colored markers may be nice for selected highlighting, but stick with black or dark blue for readability. Stay away from brands whose colors bleed onto the next sheet of paper. Bring your own; those provided in meeting rooms are often on their last legs.

23. Don't use flip charts for large audiences.

When attendance exceeds seventy-five, overhead transparencies are better for those sitting in the back rows.

If you rely on a model or handouts:

24. Never circulate a 3-D model through the audience.

Conversation will follow it throughout the room. Instead, place the model on a table in front of the audience and refer to it as you talk.

25. Do not attempt to speak while handouts are being passed out or while people are reading them.

Wait until they can give you their full attention.

26. **Never pass out a printed handout that does not pertain directly to your talk.**

Distribute supplemental material in the back of the room at the end of your talk.

#24
Twelve Techniques for Conducting a Successful Question-and-Answer Session

1. **Look directly at the person asking the question; then direct your answer to the entire audience.**
   Don't engage in dialogues.
2. **Listen carefully to all questions.**
   Concentrate on both verbal and nonverbal cues. (5, 8)
3. **Be sure you understand the question.**
   Seek clarification; ask for the question to be repeated.
4. **Repeat questions for large audiences.**
   Make sure everyone hears the question; give yourself time to think.
5. **Refer to visual aids to reinforce your answers.**
   Bring more documentation than you will need for the speech itself. Have some in reserve.
6. **Do not allow one person to monopolize.**
   Turn away from the monopolizer and call on others. If the monopolizer is someone you must appease, then grin and bear it.
7. **If you don't have an answer to a specific question, don't fake it.**
   Promise to follow up on the question and get the answer quickly.
8. **Keep the focus on the purpose of your speech.**
   Don't allow questions to divert you from your main thrust. Don't hesitate to say, "That's interesting, but beyond the scope of my presentation."

9. **Retain control of the session.**

   Don't let others use your Q & A as a personal forum. Ask debaters to rephrase assertions as questions. Never answer opinions—only questions.

10. **Respond to challenges and objections with data, not emotion.**

    Remain calm and collected. You'll win, and the hothead will lose in the audience's eyes.

11. **Know your "Achilles' Heel."**

    Plan responses for the questions you hope no one will ask.

12. **Conclude by drawing attention back to your speech's purpose.**

    Remind the audience of what you want them to do.

#25
Seven Alternative Strategies for Dealing with a Disruptive Audience

1. **Mention the names of talkers in an example that fits into your speech.**

   Say the names loudly and distinctly. You'll almost certainly get their attention and send them a private message to shut up.

2. **Move toward disruptors.**

   If you can get into the audience, enter the personal space of disruptors (about five feet away). They'll get the message without you having to say anything.

3. **Ask the entire audience for quiet.**

   Most people will know whom you mean to chastise.

4. **Stop talking.**

   At the same time look in the direction of the distractors. If this doesn't work right away, people in the audience will soon be hushing the distractors.

5. **Do nothing.**
   Wait for audience members to get upset enough to quiet the troublemakers themselves.
6. **Startle the entire audience.**
   Punch out a particular word into the microphone, or create some other aural or visual surprise that gets everyone's attention, including the distractors'.
7. **As a last resort, embarrass the distractors.**
   Ask them a question relating to your topic; ask them directly to behave properly; make a joke about them.

#26
Eighty Quotes to Enliven Your Talks

1. No matter how much cats fight there always seems to be plenty of kittens. *Abraham Lincoln*
2. The time to relax is when you don't have time for it.
   Sidney J. Harris
3. Sixty years ago I knew everything; now I know nothing. Education is the progressive discovery of our own ignorance. *Will Durant*
4. Every man has a right to his opinion. But no man has a right to be wrong in his facts. *Bernard Baruch*
5. I cannot give you the formula for success. But I can give you the formula for failure. Try to please everybody. *Herbert Bayard Swope*
6. The louder he talked of his honor, the faster we counted our spoons. *Ralph Waldo Emerson*
7. Everybody is ignorant, only on different subjects.
   Will Rogers
8. Knowledge is the only instrument of production that is not subject to diminishing returns. *J. M. Clark*
9. My mistake was buying stock in the company. Now I worry about the lousy work I'm turning out.
   Marvin Townsend

10. You can observe a lot just by watching.

Yogi Berra

11. If you don't throw it, they can't hit it.   *Lefty Gomez*

12. The race is not always to the swift nor the battle to the strong, but that's the way to bet.   *Damon Runyon*

13. Life is like a game of cards. The hand that is dealt you represents determinism; how you play it represents free will.   *Jawaharlal Nehru*

14. The only things that evolve by themselves in an organization are disorder, friction, and malperformance.

Peter Drucker

15. There are two times in a man's life when he should not speculate; when he can't afford it and when he can.   *Mark Twain*

16. There is a correlation between the creative and the screwball. So we must suffer the screwball gladly.

Kingman Brewster

17. Too bad that all the people who know how to run the country are busy driving taxicabs and cutting hair.

George Burns

18. The closest to perfection a person ever becomes is when he fills out a job application form.

Stanley J. Randall

19. In times like these, it helps to recall that there have always been times like these.   *Paul Harvey*

20. A great many people think they are thinking when they are merely rearranging their prejudices.

William James

21. Success is a matter of luck. Ask any failure.

Earl Wilson

22. Don't worry about avoiding temptation—as you grow older it starts avoiding you.

The Old Farmer's Almanac

23. The definition of a good speech is an introduction and a conclusion placed not too far apart.

Anonymous

24. Good ideas are not adopted automatically. They must be driven into practice with courageous patience.

Hyman Rickover

25. To lead, one must follow. *Lao Tzu*

26. The successful leader knows the way, shows the way, and goes the way. *Anonymous*

27. The leader must know, must know that he knows, and must be able to make it abundantly clear to those about him that he knows. *Clarence B. Randall*

28. Minds are like parachutes. They only function when they are open. *Thomas Dewar*

29. When the eyes say one thing, and the tongue another, a practised man relies on the language of the first.

Ralph Waldo Emerson

30. Quarrels would not last long if the fault was only on one side. *François de la Rochefoucauld*

31. Few people know how to hold a meeting. Even fewer know how to let it go. *Robert Fuoss*

32. A soft answer turneth away wrath. *Proverbs*

33. The final test of a leader is that he leaves behind him in other men the conviction and the will to carry on.

Walter Lippmann

34. Some people will never learn anything because they understand everything too soon. *Anonymous*

35. A good ad should be like a good sermon: it must not only comfort the afflicted—it also must afflict the comfortable. *Bernice Fitz-Gibbon*

36. If the trumpet give an uncertain sound, who shall prepare himself to the battle? *1 Corinthians*

37. When I'm getting ready to reason with a man I spend one third of the time thinking about myself—what I'm going to say—and two thirds thinking about him and what he is going to say. *Abraham Lincoln*

38. Go put your creed into your deed.

Ralph Waldo Emerson

39. A diamond is a chunk of coal made good under pressure. *Anonymous*

40. If the blind lead the blind, both shall fall into the ditch. *Matthew*

41. A new idea is delicate. It can be killed by a sneer or a yawn; it can be stabbed to death by a quip and worried to death by a frown on the right man's brow.

Charles Browner

42. He can best be described as one of those orators who, before they get up, do not know what they are going to say; when they are speaking, do not know what they are saying; and, when they have sat down, do not know what they have said. *Winston Churchill*

43. The harder the conflict, the more glorious the triumph. *Thomas Paine*

44. Beware of the man who knows the answer before he understands the question. *C. M. Manasco*

45. How many a dispute could have been deflated into a single paragraph if the disputants had dared to define their terms. *Aristotle*

46. It is just as important to listen to someone with your eyes as it is with your ears. *Martin Buxbaum*

47. It is not best that we should all think alike; it is difference of opinion which makes horse races.

Mark Twain

48. A certain amount of opposition is a great help to a man. Kites rise against, not with, the wind.

John Neal

49. How many men think of improving their talk as well as their golf handicap? *F. L. Lucas*

50. A committee of three gets things done if two don't show up. *Herbert V. Prochnow*

51. Blessed is the man who, having nothing to say, abstains from giving wordy evidence of the fact.

George Eliot

52. If Moses had been a committee, Israel would still be in Egypt.   *Anonymous*

53. No man would listen to you talk if he didn't know it was his turn next.   *E. W. Howe*

54. If your lips would keep from slips, five things observe with care: to whom you speak; of whom you speak; and how, and when, and where.

William Edward Norris

55. Never praise a sister, to a sister, in the hopes of your compliment reaching the proper ears.

Rudyard Kipling

56. A speech is like a love affair. Any fool can start it, but to end it requires considerable skill.   *Lord Mancroft*

57. My father gave me these hints of speech making: be sincere . . . be brief . . . be seated.   *James Roosevelt*

58. Never, for the sake of peace and quiet, deny your own experience or convictions.   *Dag Hammerskjold*

59. Those of us who keep our eyes open can read volumes into what we see going on around us.   *Edward Hall*

60. Employees react to management's behavior and not to its protestations.   *Saul Gellerman*

61. If a man does not know to what port he is steering, no wind is favorable to him.   *Seneca*

62. He who knows, yet thinks that he does not know, has great wisdom. He who does not know and thinks he knows is diseased.   *Lao Tzu*

63. Being powerful is like being a lady. If you have to tell people you are, you ain't.   *Anonymous*

64. A boss is a person who is always early when you're late and late when you're early.   *Anonymous*

65. To know ourselves diseased is half our cure.

Alexander Pope

66. The world is not interested in the storms you encountered, but whether you brought in the ship.

Anonymous

67. One advantage of talking to yourself is that you know at least somebody's listening. *Anonymous*

68. From the discontent of man the world's best progress springs. *Ella Wheeler Wilcox*

69. When elephants fight, it's the grass that suffers. *African proverb*

70. There are no facts, only interpretations. *Friedrich Nietzsche*

71. Some problems never get solved; they just get older. *Anonymous*

72. Trouble creates a capacity to handle it. *Oliver Wendell Holmes, Jr.*

73. Compromise is the art of dividing a cake in such a way that everyone believes he got the biggest piece. *Anonymous*

74. Animals, like human beings, have to be encouraged, petted, and above all, made to feel important if they are to do their best work. *Anonymous*

75. All progress has resulted from people who took unpopular positions. *Adlai Stevenson*

76. One of the best ways to persuade others is with your ears—by listening to them. *Dean Rusk*

77. The best thing to do behind a person's back is pat it. *Anonymous*

78. Use what talents you possess—the woods would be very silent if no birds sang there except those that sang best. *Henry VanDyke*

79. Few things help an individual more than to place responsibility upon him and to let him know that you trust him. *Booker T. Washington*

80. He that complies against his will is of his own opinion still. *Samuel Butler*

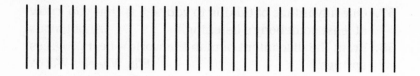

3. Write for Results

WHY IS IT that smart executives, who often possess advanced degrees from highly respected universities, send out memos, reports, and letters fraught with misspellings, incorrect grammar, improper usage, awkward construction, and numbing prose? Why are business letters specifically and business writing generally so dismal? And why are "Effective Business Writing" seminars a growing industry?

You will hear different answers to these questions depending on whom you ask. Sociologists and cultural anthropologists tell us that television has transformed us from a print to a visual society. They mourn for children in homes with larger collections of videotapes than books. Some professional educators blame the era of permissiveness that supported self-designed majors and courses where relevance was more important than fundamentals. They could point to the many high schools in this country that offer driver's education but not Latin.

Business executives themselves complain that they were simply too busy to take advanced composition courses in college. Marketing, finance, accounting, and management are studies directly related to the bottom line; writing is not. Besides, grammar and spelling checkers will help overcome writing weaknesses and correct errors.

These three responses show there are explanations for

the poor state of business writing. Nevertheless, we shouldn't accept this state of affairs as something over which we have no control. We have both the responsibility and the ability to effect change in ourselves and in our writing skills. The lists in this chapter focus your attention on your ability to write clearly and correctly.

Someone once said that whenever you communicate you're saying three things: something about your message, something about your reader, and something about yourself. When you write clearly you're showing that you understand the reader, you've thought clearly about your purpose and have expressed it well, and you're presenting a positive image of yourself.

When you write clearly and achieve these three purposes you will also enjoy one other outcome: your bottom line will be improved. That's right. Clear written communication saves time, frustration, and inconvenience—all of which represent costs. So, study the lists and start working on your bottom line.

#27
Ten Tips for Overcoming Writer's Block

1. **Jot down any idea that comes to you, whenever it comes to you.**
   Use a place mat, an envelope, or any scrap of paper available when you think of a good idea. Don't assume that you'll remember it later. A sentence, a phrase, a word, even a rough diagram or chart will be useful when your deadline approaches and you have to write.
2. **"Think out loud" about your topic.**
   Talk about it to a colleague, relative, or friend. Use a tape recorder and make notes of what was said. Getting some notes on paper this way will get you over the hurdle of facing that blank page.

3. **Create a "profile" of your topic.**

   Write a one sentence answer to the following questions. What am I writing about? What do I want my reader to do about it? What does my reader need to know in order to respond? How can I convince my reader? The answers will give you the core of your report.

4. **"Send a cable" to your reader.**

   Pretend your reader is out of the country, so you have to send your message by cablegram. Words are money, so you want to be brief but clear. Your "cable" may help you identify the key points you need to make in your report.

5. **Try a "three-minute overseas phone call."**

   With tape recorder and timer running, give your report to the person at the other end of the "phone" in three minutes or less.

6. **Use journalism's "five W's and an H" technique.**

   Answer the questions "who," "what," "where," "when," "why," and "how" for your subject. Then rearrange or reword your answers into an outline you can work from.

7. **Brainstorm a map of all the central ideas you need to cover.**

   Don't worry yet about their order; just write them down as you think of them. A good way to do this is to jot your writing purpose in the center of a large sheet of paper. Write central ideas as you think of them on lines emanating out of the statement of purpose in all directions. Don't attempt to organize these ideas until you get them all onto this "cognitive map." (11)

8. **Write the introduction *after* you write the rest of the piece.**

   The introduction is a forecast of what is to come, but most people refine and recast their ideas as they write. So it's often more efficient to write the introduction after you've finished and can see what you actually did.

9. **Write the conclusion *first*.**

By writing your concluding sentence, paragraph, or section first, you may see more clearly how to organize your points to get to that conclusion. You can revise it later, if necessary.

10. **Don't try to write finished prose as you go.**

Your first goal is to get your thoughts and ideas on paper, regardless of word choice, sentence structure, or spelling. Word processing makes it easy to polish your prose later. Get it written before you worry about getting it right.

#28

Ten Techniques to Improve Your Letters' "Personality"

1. **Ask yourself, "Would I *say* what I've written?"**

Read it aloud. If you think it sounds stuffy or artificial, it is.

2. **Be concise.**

Don't use long, wordy phrases when a single word will do. Why say "at this point in time" when you can say "now"?

3. **Don't create long, complex sentences by connecting phrase after phrase with "and."**

Don't write, "I am enrolled in the Master of Business Administration Program of Ourtown University in Ourtown, California, and I will be graduating with my MBA degree in June, and am interested in working for your company." Give the reader some breathing space: "I am enrolled in the Master of Business Administration Program of Ourtown University in Ourtown, California. I will be graduating with my MBA degree in June, and am interested in working for your company."

4. **If a one-syllable word will do the job, use it.**

   There is no need to say you "desire" a position in international finance when you can simply say that you "want" one. Don't "inquire" about a job; just "ask" about it.

5. **Use powerful, colorful words that create a mental picture for your reader.**

   A writer who is "excited" or "eager" about a career in finance sounds more energetic than one who is merely "interested." When you tell a reader you are "tackling" a problem, the term evokes the strong, assertive image of a football game.

6. **Write with a "*you*" attitude, not with a "*me*" attitude.**

   Put yourself in your reader's chair and focus on that person's goals and concerns rather than on your own. For example, tell a potential employer what you can do to further the organization's goals, not what you expect the organization to do for you.

7. **Pay attention to title and rank.**

   If your reader has a professional designation or title, such as doctor or professor, use it in the address. People are proud of their professional achievements and are likely to respond positively to a writer who recognizes them.

8. **Use friendly language.**

   You can use contractions such as "I'll" for "I will" or "wouldn't" for "would not" in all but the most formal writing situations.

9. **Avoid clichés.**

   If you have to deliver bad news, it doesn't help to assure your reader that "every cloud has a silver lining." A leader adept at motivating subordinates needn't be called a "people person."

10. **Use specific examples to bring your points to life.**

Instead of asserting that you're "well qualified for the job," cite the specific courses and work experience that make you well qualified.

#29
Seven Tips for Convincing Your Reader

1. **Explain something new or unfamiliar to your reader by comparing it with something that person already knows.**

For example, compare the features of a proposed new office system with those of an existing one, to show how the new one would handle tasks that the reader is familiar with.

2. **Provide evidence to back up your generalizations and conclusions.**

Evidence can take the following forms: statistics, statements from a recognized expert or authority, official or legal definitions or regulations, and demonstrations of cause and effect. Don't assume that evidence is unnecessary because your reader has access to the same information you do. If your reader's stake in the issue is different from yours, the same information may be interpreted differently.

3. **Avoid vague words such as "faster" or "better."**

How fast is "faster"? "Better" than what? It's much more convincing to say that your plan "will reduce waiting time by two minutes per customer." If you don't have the information you need to make a specific statement, you're not ready to write.

4. **Write for your reader, not for yourself.**

You know where you're going, but your reader needs some traffic signals and landmarks along the way. Provide them in the form of headings, illustrations, and clear transitions from one point to the next. Readers don't like unexpected detours or surprise endings.

5. **Make your writing easy to read.**

   Break long paragraphs into shorter ones, list separate elements or features, and provide generous margins.

6. **Illustrate the relationships among people, tasks, or numbers.**

   For example, show reporting relationships by means of an organization chart, show work flows with a flow chart, and show percentages on a pie chart. The old adage that "a picture is worth a thousand words" is particularly true for data of this type.

7. **Summarize your major points and restate your purpose at the end of memos, reports, or letters that are longer than one page.**

   The ending should remind your reader that you had a good reason for writing.

#30
Eleven Ways to Create More Persuasive Letters

1. **Plan before you write.**

   Answer these questions: What do I hope to accomplish with this letter? Who is my reader, and what does he or she need to know? What circumstances affect the approach I need to take? What additional information do I need before I start writing? Visualize the entire letter before writing.

2. **Use the "you" approach.**

   Readers would rather read about themselves than about you. Refer to them whenever possible. Instead of "Our new software package saves the consumer $500," write, "You will save $500 with our new software package."

3. **Use positive statements.**

   Most people would rather hear positive words than negative ones. Change "I don't mind accepting the assignment" to "I accept the assignment."

4. **Use powerful words.**

   Create a picture in the reader's mind. Powerful words are *short* ("use" is stronger than "utilize"), *specific* ("Cadillac" is stronger than "car"), *concise* ("I plan to quit" is stronger than "I am planning to quit"), *compact* ("scribbled" is stronger than "wrote hastily"), *familiar* ("hardened" is stronger than "sclerous"), and *unexpected* ("pieces" might be profitably changed to "fragments").

5. **Eliminate unnecessary words.**

   Carefully go over your rough draft for all words that can be removed without weakening the message. "Editing [is a process that] removes [all those] unnecessary words that take [up large amounts of extra] space but add nothing [of any real significance] to the [meaning of the] message."

6. **Catch your reader's attention in the opening paragraph.**

   Your reader will judge from the opening paragraph whether to read on. In some cases, that's all that will be read. Attempt to cover "who, what, where, when, why, and how" as early as possible.

7. **State good news at the beginning of the letter.**

   Don't keep your reader guessing when you have good news to share.

8. **Withhold bad news until the end of the letter.**

   By delaying the explicit statement of bad news, you allow emotional space for the reader to anticipate and better accept the disappointing message.

9. **Convince your reader with evidence.**

   Mere restatements of your initial assertion won't do. Provide specific examples; state verifiable facts; quote reliable, properly identified statistics; cite expert testimony; quote official definitions; make comparisons to things the reader already knows.

10. **Close with a statement of actions to be taken.**

   If you want the reader to do something or if you are going to do something, say exactly that in the final paragraph. Don't beat around the bush or bury actions in the middle of the letter where they won't have impact.

11. **Sign your name in blue ink.**

   If your letter is typed in black your signature will stand out, emphasizing the personal nature of the communication.

#31

Thirteen Common Grammatical Errors to Avoid

1. ***Don't* write or say "between you and I."**

   The correct form is "between you and me." "Between" is a preposition like "with" or "from," so it needs the objective pronoun "me." Just as we say "I am going" but "she is going with me," we say "you and I know this," but "between you and me."

2. ***Don't* write "alot."**

   The correct form is two words, "a lot."

3. ***Don't* write "all ready," except as in "we were all ready for the presentation to begin."**

   "Already" is the correct form of the adverb meaning "by this time." "He had already explained the report when I arrived, so the committee was all ready to decide."

4. ***Don't* confuse the contraction "it's" with the possessive "its."**

   "It's" is a contraction for "it is." "Its" is a possessive

pronoun. "When you look at that chair, it's obvious that one of its legs is shorter than the other."

5. ***Don't* confue the plural form "companies" with the possessive form "company's."**

"'The customer is always right' is my company's motto, but many other companies act as if their motto were, 'Let the buyer beware.'"

6. ***Don't* use "loose" when you mean "lose."**

When you lose your wallet, it is lost. When you loosen your tie, it is not so tight. "Children's teeth become loose before they lose them."

7. ***Don't* confuse "their," "there," and "they're."**

"Their" is possessive, as in "Sue and John invited us to their house." "There" is a location, as in "Sue and John's house? I've been there." "They're" is a contraction for "they are," as in "They're such nice hosts, aren't they?"

8. ***Don't* put an apostrophe before an "s" that is part of the basic word or name.**

The car that Joan Richards owns is Joan Richards's car, not Joan Richard's car, because her name is Richards, not Richard.

9. ***Don't* use dangling phrases.**

A phrase is left dangling if it is impossible to connect it to the subject of a sentence: "By blinking, the contact lens will center itself over the cornea." The contact lens can't blink, but the wearer should, so the instruction should read: "Blink to center the contact lens on the cornea," or "Blink. The contact lens will center itself on the cornea."

10. ***Don't* use singular verbs with plural subjects or vice versa.**

Say, "The costs of producing and distributing the product are high," or, "The cost of producing and distributing the product is high," but *not,* "The cost of producing and distributing the product are high."

11. **_Don't_ use "their" when a singular pronoun is correct.**

Don't say, "Each employee must complete their evaluation form." Say, "Each employee must complete his or her evaluation form," or, "All employees must complete their evaluation forms."

12. **_Don't_ use a comma to string together two clauses when each could be a sentence on its own.**

Use a semicolon or make each a separate sentence. Incorrect: "We increased our productivity by 20 percent, therefore, we think we deserve a raise." Correct: "We increased our productivity by 20 percent; therefore, we think we deserve a raise." Also correct: "We increased our productivity by 20 percent. Therefore, we think we deserve a raise."

13. **_Don't_ separate the subject and verb of a sentence with a comma.**

Incorrect: "Those who have not taken their vacations by December 31, will forfeit any unused days." Correct: "Those who have not taken their vacations by December 31 will forfeit any unused days."

#32
Fifteen Commonly Confused Words

1. **Affect or effect?**

As a verb, _effect_ means "to bring about" or "to accomplish," while _affect_ means "to influence." "The manager sought to affect her employees positively by effecting a new promotion policy."

2. **Allude or elude?**

You _allude_ to the document where a fact may be found; you _elude_ a question that you cannot answer.

3. **Can or may?**

   Can refers to ability; *may* refers to permission. "I can run a meeting. May I lead your meeting?"

4. **Comprise or constitute?**

   A team *comprises* the people who work on it, but people do not comprise a team; they *constitute* the team.

5. **Disinterested or uninterested?**

   Disinterested means "impartial," as in, "The mediator was called in as a disinterested third party." *Uninterested* means "not interested in," as in, "That candidate was uninterested in our job offer."

6. **Farther or further?**

   Farther is more appropriate as a distance word, as in, "We walked farther than we usually do." *Further* works best as a term of time or quantity, as in, "We pursued the topic further than anyone had previously."

7. **Finalize or complete?**

   Don't fall into the common trap of coining verbs by tacking "-ize" onto words. Business writers and speakers are especially guilty of such errors as "finalize," "customize," and "prioritize."

8. **Good or well?**

   In reporting conditions such as health or performance, write, "I am feeling well," or, "She performed well." In such situations, never substitute the adjective "good" for the adverb "well." When describing attitude, it is proper to say, "I feel good today."

9. **Imply or infer?**

   When you *imply*, you indicate or suggest something by word or action, without actually saying it. When you *infer*, you deduce or draw a conclusion from the evidence.

10. **Irregardless or regardless?**

    Irregardless is incorrect.

11. Lay or lie?

Do not misuse the transitive verb *lay when the* intransitive verb *lie* is correct. "The manager lays an egg with his boss; the manager lies down." But *lay* is also the past tense of *lie*: "The employee went home and lay down."

12. Precede or proceed?

When you go ahead or in front of, you *precede*. When you begin or carry on some action, you *proceed*. "Because I preceded everyone else in line at the deli counter, I proceeded to give my order when the clerk asked who was next."

13. Principle or principal?

A *principal* is the head of a school, a chief official, or an original sum (as in a loan). When used as an adjective it means, "of primary importance." A *principle* is a fundamental truth. "As a principal of the firm, Neil was obliged to adhere to a rigid set of ethical principles."

14. Oral or verbal?

Verbal refers to words either written or spoken; *oral* refers to the mouth. "Oral agreement" is more precise than "verbal agreement" to mean that a contract is not consummated in writing.

15. Than or then?

Than is used in comparisons: "Stacy is more sensitive to subordinates than Fran." *Then* indicates temporal sequence: "She revised her résumé, then sent it out to prospective employers."

#33
Fifty Frequently Misspelled Words

1. Accommodate
2. Acknowledgment
3. Acquaintance
4. Already

5. Apologize
6. Beginning
7. Benefited
8. Canceled
9. Commitment
10. Committee
11. Conscientious
12. Consensus
13. Deferred
14. Definite
15. Dilemma
16. Disappoint
17. Eligible
18. Embarrass
19. Existence
20. Extension
21. Foreign
22. Government
23. Grateful
24. Harass
25. Incidentally
26. Inconvenience
27. Necessary

28. Noticeable
29. Occasion
30. Occurrence
31. Occurred
32. Omission
33. Omitted
34. Personnel
35. Possession
36. Precede
37. Privilege
38. Procedure
39. Professor
40. Questioner
41. Questionnaire
42. Receive
43. Recommend
44. Referred
45. Separate
46. Similar
47. Sincerely
48. Tomorrow
49. Transferring
50. Unnecessary

#34
Nine Techniques for Overcoming Sexist Language

1. **Where you use "Mr." for a man, use "Ms." for a woman.**
   If possible, though, check to see if the woman prefers "Miss" or "Mrs."
2. **Don't assume that someone listed by initials is male.**
   If the listing is "A. B. Jones," address your letter to "Dear A. B. Jones," not "Dear Mr. Jones."

3. **When you refer to men and women who are professional peers, use the same form of name for all.**

   It's "John, Jim, and Jane," not "Mr. Jones, Mr. Woods, and Jane," nor "John, Jim, and Miss Smith."

4. **Address a woman by her professional title.**

   A dentist named Smith is Dr. Smith regardless of gender or social situation. Your Christmas card can be addressed to Dr. Jane Smith and Mr. William Smith (if she has that title and he does not) or to Jane and William Smith or William and Jane Smith, but not to Mr. and Mrs. William Smith.

5. **Avoid the "generic he" when you mean a man *or* woman.**

   Don't say, "Each employee must complete his evaluation by December 31." Use "his or her," or—better still—use the plural: "Employees must complete their evaluations by December 31."

6. **Find substitutes for "-man" and "-men" word endings.**

   Say "firefighter" instead of "fireman," "mail carrier" instead of "mailman," "managers" or "business executives" or "business owners" instead of "businessmen."

7. **To avoid overusing "person," turn nouns into verbs.**

   Instead of "Sally Smith is chairperson of the committee," you can say, "Sally Smith chairs the committee." Or use "people" instead of "persons" or "men," as in "We need more salespeople during the holiday season."

8. **Don't use the "-ess" ending to designate a woman.**

   Rosabeth Moss Kanter is the author (not the authoress) of *The Change Masters.*

9. **Avoid the term "girl" (as in "the girls in the office").**

   Ask yourself if you would use "boy" in the equivalent situation. If not, find another term, such as "the office staff."

#35
Fourteen Good References for Writers

1. **American Heritage Dictionary of the English Language: Third Edition.**
   Houghton-Mifflin Company, Boston, 1992.
2. **The Business Writer's Handbook, by Charles T. Brusaw, Gerald J. Alred, and Walter E. Oliu.**
   St. Martin's Press, New York, 1997.
3. **The Elements of Style, by William Strunk, Jr. and E. B. White.**
   Prentice-Hall, New York, 1979.
4. **The Handbook of Non-Sexist Writing, by Casey Miller and Kate Swift.**
   HarperCollins, New York, 1992.
5. **The Little, Brown Handbook, by H. Ramsey Fowler.**
   Addison-Wesley, Reading, Massachusetts, 1997.
6. **The Little English Handbook, by Edward Corbett.**
   Addison-Wesley, Reading, Massachusetts, 1997.
7. **Peter's Quotations, by Laurence Peter.**
   Morrow, New York, 1993.
8. **Reporting Technical Information, by Kenneth W. Houp and Thomas E. Pearsall.**
   Prentice-Hall, New York, 1997.
9. **The St. Martin's Guide to Writing (Short Edition), by Rise B. Axelrod and Charles R. Cooper.**
   St. Martin's Press, New York, 1994.
10. **Webster's Collegiate Thesaurus.**
    Merriam-Webster Inc., Springfield, Massachusetts, 1988.
11. **Words at Work: Business Writing in Half the Time with Twice the Power, by Susan Benjamin.**
    Addison-Wesley, Reading, Massachusetts, 1997.

12. **Writing: A Guide for Business Professionals,** by **C. W. Griffin.**
Harcourt Brace Jovanovich, San Diego, 1987.

13. **Writing Skills for Bankers, by Mildred S. Myers.**
American Bankers Association, Washington, D.C., 1992.

14. **The Internet.**
Bookmark a general reference page that will link you to style manuals, quotation collections, and other valuable sites.

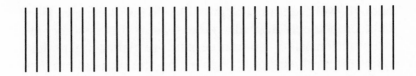

4. Supervise Assertively

IN ONE OF our recent seminars, an experienced manager employed by a *Fortune* 500 company complained about his job: "You know, this would be a wonderful place to work if it weren't for the people who work here." You may have had the same feelings at times.

Why is it that managers across all industries and across all levels of the hierarchy often voice this complaint? The answer is simple: often managers are promoted solely because they know the technical aspects of their job extremely well. However, once they're in a management position, technical skills become less important and interpersonal skills become more important. Managers without them quickly become frustrated with the complex interactions they now face with others throughout the organization. This is especially true for their relationships with subordinates, a new animal for many first-time managers.

Competent technicians promoted to management positions soon learn that knowing how to do something and getting others to do it are two drastically different skills. The satisfaction they once felt in performing a task is replaced by the frustration of getting others to do it—sometimes reluctantly.

A few years ago, Laurence J. Peter wrote a best-seller, *The Peter Principle*, which expanded on how technical skills won't compensate for lack of interpersonal skills. Its central thesis was that every manager, if promoted often enough, will eventually be promoted to his or her own level of incompetence. Basically, Peter tells us that past technical proficiency is no guarantee of future managerial performance, and if we promote solely on the basis of current technical competence, we will eventually put people into positions where they will be unable to handle the challenge. The antidote for managerial incompetence? Acquiring those new skills and abilities demanded by the future.

The lists in this section are based both on this simple principle and on the definition of management itself. That definition, often cited in management textbooks, is as follows: *management* is achieving results through the efforts of others. Each list contained in this section is designed to help you perform the management job for which you were hired or into which you were promoted.

We've labeled this section "Supervise Assertively" because we believe that achieving results through others means that you solve, rather than avoid, the human problems you're likely to confront. You can't wish them away, rationalize them away, or bury your head in the sand so that you can't see them. Neither can you succeed in the long run with an aggressive, authoritarian, "do it my way" style.

You must manage employees assertively. And when you do, you will no longer complain, "This would be a nice place if it weren't for the other people who work here." On the contrary, you will rejoice that "this is a great place *because* of the people who work here—especially those who work for me."

#36
Nineteen Strategies for Successful Leadership

1. **Maintain good relations with your boss.**
   The health of this relationship is directly reflected in

your ability to satisfy and therefore influence employees. Powerful leaders are those who get power from their bosses. (135–140)

2. **Show your employees the qualities you want them to show you.**

   Get the honesty, loyalty, sensitivity, thoughtfulness, decisiveness, flexibility, rationality, objectivity, initiative, and enthusiasm you want from subordinates by displaying these qualities yourself. Modeling is the most powerful leadership strategy.

3. **Make your expectations clearly known.**

   How else can you expect people to satisfy them? Never assume that subordinates know what behavior and results you expect of them. Never be afraid to tell them exactly what you want. Tell them *before* they do it, and as often as you can. (71)

4. **Use meetings to strengthen the team.**

   Encourage participation and idea sharing. Keep the group focused on its goals. (58–69)

5. **Reward cooperation and hard work.**

   Don't take good performance for granted. Reward it and you can expect to see a lot more of it.

6. **Accept employee differences and take advantage of them.**

   Not everyone can be a company star. Some people will prosper in jobs that cause others to stagnate. Just as you should treat each of your children as an only child, treat each of your employees as an only employee.

7. **Give feedback to individuals regarding their contribution to the team.**

   Do this objectively, honestly, and often. Make certain they know how well they are meeting your expectations and where they can improve. (41, 45)

8. **Listen to employees.**

   They will feel that what they have to say is important.

You'll gain their respect and loyalty. You'll also learn more of what's going on. (4, 5)

9. *Hire* **team players.**

No amount of training will convert an inadequate or alienated employee into a winner for you. Screen candidates carefully. Don't waste dollars trying to reform mistakes; leave that to your competitor. (95)

10. **Share your goals, visions, motivations, and reasons.**

Don't tell people what to do. Tell them what your needs are in the situation, and let them help you decide the best way of meeting those needs.

11. **Admit your mistakes.**

Rather than being a sign of weakness, this is a sign of strength.

12. **Don't promise—deliver.**

Only two things can happen when you make a promise, and neither one of them is very good. A fulfilled promise is *expected;* an unfulfilled promise can end a relationship.

13. **Manage your time well.**

Free as much time as possible to spend with employees. (118–125)

14. **Put people into jobs where they are most likely to meet their own needs as well as those of the organization.**

This is the best single answer to the question, "How do I motivate my employees?"

15. **Do the little things that show subordinates you value them as individuals.**

You know what makes *you* feel good. Chances are the same things will work with them. People want to feel important; if you oblige them, they'll oblige you. (42)

16. **Approach disagreements honestly and squarely.**

Be aware of the results of your conflict resolution style; learn to use conflict positively. (70–80)

17. **Give people the information they need to do their job—before they need it.**

For many employees, information is one of the necessary resources that's in short supply. When you delegate a job, make available all of your information on it. (38)

18. **Periodically disengage from day-to-day pressures.**

You'll gain time to think about how well goals are being achieved and what plans should be made. Otherwise, you'll spend most of your time fighting fires and putting grease only on the squeaky wheels. (111, 118)

19. **Don't take yourself too seriously.**

Laugh at yourself and with your people.

#37
Nine Ways to Develop Your Subordinates

1. **Assign important, challenging jobs.**

Cut them loose on risky projects. Give them a chance to show what they can do.

2. **Gradually mete out responsibility for tasks you usually perform personally.**

This develops them while freeing you for greater challenges. (38)

3. **Praise employees when they have performed a job well.**

They will be more motivated if they know that you appreciate their efforts. (48, 54)

4. **Involve them in decision making—solicit their suggestions.**

5. **Send them to a management development or personal enrichment seminar once a year.**

Attending seminars makes people feel important and it teaches them new skills. (106, 107)

6. **Provide frequent, honest, and objective feedback.**
The periodic formal performance appraisal should not contain surprise information. Don't defer praise or reprimands until then. (41–43, 45–47, 108)

7. **Don't solve problems for them.**
Teach them how to solve problems for themselves.

8. **Remain accessible for their problems or questions.**
Keep an open door and an open mind.

9. **Train your subordinates so that one or more of them can take over your job when you leave or get promoted.**
Your replacement should be working for you right now. (100)

#38

Ten Rules for Delegation

1. **Make sure the employee has the skill, talent, and ability to perform the job.**
Don't delegate a job destined to result in failure or frustration.

2. **Check with your boss.**
Unless you have been given complete discretion in this matter, be certain the boss agrees to your giving up a particular responsibility.

3. **Delegate not only the menial, unimportant jobs but also the significant ones.**
Employees will see this as a vote of confidence.

4. **Make sure subordinates clearly understand the task.**
Have subordinates describe what they think you want them to accomplish. (3)

5. **Allow the subordinate latitude in how the job should be performed.**
Your way is *not* the only way. However, if there are

rules or constraints which must be followed, make sure you communicate them.

6. **Provide *all* the resources necessary to perform the job.**
   If you're going to delegate, also provide the necessary help.

7. **Remain accessible.**
   Always provide a "safety net" for the subordinate. Be available, but don't engage in over-the-shoulder surveillance.

8. **If the job is performed well, praise the subordinate.** (42, 43, 54)

9. **If not, tell your subordinate how to improve.** (45, 46)

10. **Delegate often—everyone wins.**

#39
Seven Tips for Increasing Upward Communication

1. **Practice MBWA—Managing By Wandering Around.**
   Find out what's happening among your people. Don't talk; just ask questions and listen. (5)

2. **Maintain an "open-door policy."**
   Let your employees know that if they ever have a problem, they can come and see you.

3. **Tell your employees that the *only* bad news is the news that is not communicated upward.**
   Tell them that you want to hear the good news *and* the bad news.

4. **Don't react badly when you hear that something is amiss.**
   Don't "kill" the bearer of bad tidings.

5. **Arrange for periodic informal gatherings.**
   Have picnics, parties, group lunches. People will tell

you things at a picnic they won't tell you in your office. Attending social gatherings makes you more accessible.

6. **At staff meetings, solicit regular status reports.**

   Don't be overly judgmental of what you hear in these reports.

7. **Show that you're human.**

   Laugh at yourself, admit your mistakes, apologize if you've done something to hurt an employee. If they think you're human, you will be more approachable.

#40
Nine Prescriptions for Giving Job Instructions

1. **Set aside time in a quiet place so that you can give instructions without distractions.**

   Don't give them on the run or piecemeal.

2. **Anticipate the employee's feelings, needs, and concerns.**

   If you once held the job, remember what it felt like and the problems you had understanding complex instructions from your boss.

3. **Ask the employee to tell you what he or she currently knows about the job.**

   Fill in the gaps so that your instructions will be understood.

4. **Use simple, concrete, and specific language.**

   Avoid jargon if possible. Speak in the language of the receiver. (3, 6)

5. **Don't belabor the obvious.**

   Talk about what they don't know, not what they do.

6. **If possible, demonstrate the correct performance of the job.**

   Show the employee how it should be done, or what it

should look like when it is done. If you cannot do this physically, try to create a vivid mental image of the completed task. Give examples.

7. **Ask the employee to try it.**
   Coach and counsel with immediate feedback. If performance is incorrect, tell why and provide another model of appropriate performance. If it's done correctly, praise the employee.

8. **Ask the employee if he or she has any questions.**
   Respond courteously to all questions. Don't belittle an employee for asking what you think is a stupid question.

9. **Tell the employee you'll remain accessible when problems or other questions arise.**
   Make sure you can be easily reached, even by the shyest or most insecure employee.

#41

Eleven Steps for Conducting an Effective Performance Appraisal

1. **Let your subordinate prepare.**
   A week before the appraisal tell the subordinate to engage in a careful self-analysis of his or her performance during the preceding performance period.

2. **Set aside at least 45 minutes of uninterrupted time.**

3. **At the beginning of the session put the subordinate at ease.**
   Performance appraisals are potentially threatening to employees. Minimize the threat and the potential for defensiveness. Explain that performance reviews are simply a structured version of work-related communication. (91)

4. **Focus the appraisal on performance and behavior—not inference and personality.**

   What specifically did the employee do well or poorly? Give abundant examples. (45, 46)

5. **Deemphasize any numerical scale used on the form.**

   Discourage the employee from leaving your office as a "4." Coaching, counseling, and specific plans for improvement are more important than numerical labels. Talk about the *meaning* of the numbers, not the numbers themselves.

6. **Solicit the employee's perceptions of his or her performance.**

   If your perception and assessment differ, probe to determine why. Again, ask the employee to focus on performance and behavior, not intent or attempt.

7. **Compare performance relative to a standard or an expectation.**

   If you have failed to set the standard or expectation, rectify that immediately. Make sure that this evaluation sets the standard for the next. (71)

8. **Make sure that the employee defines terms the same way you do.**

   Ask for his or her definition and interpretation of the appraisal form, if you use one.

9. **Build coaching and counseling into the appraisal.**

   What can you do to help the employee perform better in the future?

10. **Along with the employee, develop an action plan for closing the "performance gap."**

    How can you eliminate the difference between current behavior and expected behavior? What will the employee do differently and when? (111)

11. **Conclude the interview with a clear, explicit understanding.**

    Have the employee tell you in his or her own words what will happen as a consequence of the appraisal and why. If appropriate, have the employee sign the appraisal form.

#42

Eight Reasons Supervisors Don't Give the Praise They Should

1. Some managers who *expect* the best see no need to reward it.
2. High-achieving managers may have difficulty recognizing subordinate accomplishments that do not approach their personal standards.
3. Some managers believe the stick is more motivating than the carrot.
4. People who have been raised in impersonal environments may have difficulty expressing warm, personal thanks.
5. The manager may not spend enough time with subordinates to see their significant accomplishments.
6. The organizational tradition or climate may not encourage the giving of praise.
7. Some workers are "only" doing their job, and never excel enough in the eyes of managers to warrant praise.
8. The most common excuse for praising too little is "I'm busy."

#43

Ten Situations Where Praise Won't Motivate

1. **The receiver doesn't respect the giver.**
2. **The receiver doesn't trust the giver's motives.**
   If the giver hasn't historically been a praiser, the receiver may be suspicious of such behavior.

3. **Doing a good job isn't important to the receiver (or to the giver).**
4. **The giver praises too lavishly.**
   When laid on too thick, praise loses its power.
5. **The giver praises too often.**
   If you praised everyone, every day, it would mean little.
6. **The giver praises unwillingly and therefore insincerely.**
7. **The praise is qualified or even negated, often in the same breath.**
   "I wish you could do it that way *all* the time."
8. **Praise occurs in the wrong place.**
   Some receivers will be embarrassed in public; others disappointed to receive praise privately. Sometimes coworkers become jealous when others are praised in their presence. You've got to know how your receiver will respond.
9. **The wrong behaviors are praised.**
   Don't praise performance the subordinate considers unexceptional.
10. **Receivers are dissatisfied with the conditions of their employment.**
    Praise may not be appreciated when employees feel underpaid, overworked, or mistreated. Praise works best in a basically healthy organizational climate. It is not a substitute for fair pay and decent treatment.

#44

Eleven Questions to Ask about a Performance Problem

1. **Does the employee know what the job is?**
   How do you know?

2. **Does the employee know the quality of performance expected?**
   How do you know? (71)
3. **Has the employee performed the job correctly in the past?**
   If the answer to this question is yes, the answers to questions 1 and 2 are probably also yes. A yes also suggests that some recent event may be at the root of the problem.
4. **Is something going on in the employee's life or work environment that inhibits performance?**
5. **Has the job itself changed since the last time the employee performed it?**
   If so, you may have a need for employee training, or you may discover that some aspect of the change alienated the employee.
6. **Does the employee *want* to do a good job?**
   Actually, more people want to do a good job than many managers think.
7. **Did the employee have adequate resources to perform the job?**
   Ask yourself if the employee had enough information and sufficient access to you.
8. **Does the employee lack the ability to do the job?**
   Lack of ability can usually be addressed by training or by transferring the employee to a more appropriate assignment.
9. **Is overqualification the problem?**
   Equally damaging is the situation where the employee is not sufficiently challenged by the job. Overqualification often leads to boredom and a drop in performance.
10. **Does the employee *know* he or she is not meeting your expectations?**
    Have you explicitly said so? Never assume that your general dissatisfaction has been translated by the

employee into the specifics of what he or she is, or is not, doing on the job.

11. **What might *you* be doing to contribute to the problem?**

    Ask a colleague or other observer of the situation who would tell you the truth.

#45

Fifteen Guidelines for Giving Criticism that Changes Behavior

1. **Give the criticism in private.**

   Don't run the risk of embarrassing or humiliating the receiver.

2. **Make certain the receiver is paying attention and is emotionally ready to listen.**

   Feedback not heeded is feedback not heard.

3. **Wait for the receiver to get over anger, hurt, or confusion.**

   You want the receiver to be receptive to your message.

4. **Don't communicate in anger.**

   Calm down. This is a critical time to be objective. (77)

5. **Reject the behavior, not the person.**

   Focus on what was done rather than the person's role in it.

6. **Be clear and be specific.**

   Use actual examples. Offer them even before you're asked for them. This keeps you on the offensive, rather than on the defensive.

7. **Probe for understanding with questions.**

   Make certain the receiver understands what you're saying. Find out how he or she is taking your criticism. Make certain the data and assumptions that triggered your criticism were accurate.

8. **Give criticism while the behavior is fresh in both your minds.**
   It will have the maximum impact.
9. **Be honest with yourself about your objective.**
   If your intent is to punish, the receiver will realize this (even if you don't) and will become defensive.
10. **Show understanding of and empathy for the receiver's situation.**
    This will help win the receiver's trust.
11. **Avoid communicating superiority in knowledge, power, or insight.**
    "I'm better than you" should not be in the message.
12. **Be provisional if possible; qualify your observations.**
    Don't communicate hopelessness and finality. Rather than saying, "You're always late," specify and qualify. "You weren't at your desk by 9 A.M. on three mornings this past month."
13. **Don't ascribe intent to the person's behavior.**
    "You don't want to do a good job" will just create defensiveness. Report on the behavior only. "That approach is not acceptable."
14. **Focus on behaviors the receiver can change.**
    If you can't do this, you shouldn't be giving the criticism.
15. **Don't overload the receiver with criticism to the point that it becomes threatening or creates excessive stress.**
    Do unto others. . . .

#46
Ten Steps for Successful Criticism

1. **Tell the person what event, behavior, or performance concerns you.**
   "In this morning's staff meeting, when my boss asked

for our performance figures, you spoke up just as I was opening my mouth to respond."

2. **Tell the person how the event, behavior, or performance creates a problem.**

   "I could tell by the surprised look on my boss's face that she wondered why I, her immediate subordinate, would allow one of my subordinates to answer that question. Furthermore, I didn't want the data reported in the format you chose."

3. **Tell the person how you feel about the situation.**

   "I was embarrassed in front of my boss and disappointed that you and I don't have our act together well enough to prevent something like that from happening."

4. **Ask the person to offer an explanation of anything you appear to be misperceiving.**

   "Why did you speak up when you did, rather than defer to me?" Listen to the answer.

5. **Suggest corrective action.**

   "Let's first of all agree that performance reporting is something I will handle unless we plan otherwise for a particular meeting. Let's also begin sitting across the table from each other at staff meetings so we can pass quick nonverbal cues in such situations."

6. **If possible, involve the other person in the problem-solving process.**

   "Do you have any other ideas?" Or better yet, "How can we keep this from happening again?"

7. **Secure a commitment to future action.**

   "Do you agree that this is the best way to handle our communication at staff meetings? Do you foresee any problems in carrying it out?"

8. **Describe how you value the person.**

   "Fran, you've been attending staff meetings with me for a year and a half, and this was the first time I felt anything but appreciation for your input. And I know you'll continue to be an asset there in the future."

9. **Let your words sink in.**

    Don't start talking about something else. It's often better to leave the person alone at this point, with your words echoing in his or her ears. "If you have no other questions or comments, you can get back to work."

10. **Follow up on the corrective action.**

    Make certain commitments are fulfilled. Look for the opportunity to praise the person's new behavior.

#47

Ten Rules for Reprimands

1. **Make sure your information is accurate.**

    Don't reprimand an employee without just cause.

2. **Conduct the reprimand as soon after the infraction as possible.**

    The reprimand will lose its effectiveness if too much time lapses after the infraction.

3. **Make sure you are calm before conducting the reprimand.**

    The reprimand should have a problem-solving, not an accusatory, tone. (77)

4. **Conduct the reprimand in private.**

    Never add insult to injury. Your goal is to change behavior, not to embarrass or anger the employee.

5. **Focus on specific behavior, not on generalities.**

    What *exactly* did the employee do wrong? What data do you have?

6. **Don't discriminate or act unfairly.**

    Reprimands must be firm, fair, and consistent for all employees.

7. **Provide coaching and counseling.**

    What should the employee do differently in the future?

8. **Provide motivation and encouragement.**

   Communicate optimism that the employee's work will improve and that he or she is capable of achieving higher performance.

9. **Conclude with a clear understanding by both parties.**

   What happened? Why did it happen? What will change? When? What will be the consequences of not changing?

10. **Close the book on the reprimand.**

    It's over. Treat this employee as you treat all others. Don't try to catch someone in the act—unless it's in the act of doing things correctly.

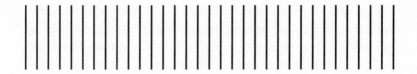

5. Create Quality

AS HISTORIANS look back at the last few decades, they are likely to describe an era when Americans stopped feeling sorry for themselves and no longer beat their breasts for being an industrial also-ran. They may look back and say the gloom and despair of the '70s changed into the hope of the twenty-first century.

The decade of the '70s inundated us with reports of deteriorating quality in American products and services, and the closing and/or restructuring of industrial giants such as U.S. Steel and International Harvester. As the '80s came to a close, American industry was making a comeback.

What happened to turn things around? American managers, whether employed in large companies or small, publicly owned or private, profit or nonprofit, woke up and realized that their international counterparts were not inherently brighter, harder working, or more motivated. However, they did realize that they and their co-workers had lost sight of the importance of quality . . . of doing it right the first time . . . of working with pride not because you're paid to do it but because that's the way to do it . . . of working with the reality that customers don't have to buy your product or service . . . of working with the standard that anything less than acceptable is not acceptable. As a nation we woke up to the reality that, unlike prior decades, good enough simply isn't good enough.

Appeals to pride, involvement, commitment, and workmanship are being heard in more and more companies at all levels of the hierarchy. And just as the single word "excellence" captured the spirit of American managers in the Peters and Waterman book, *In Search of Excellence,* we believe that a single word came to capture their pride, involvement, commitment, and workmanship. That word is *quality.*

The lists in this section represent advice on how you can implement quality in your personal work, in your group's work, or in your entire organization. Before you begin reading and applying these lists, however, we offer one precaution: prepare for the long haul. Quality cannot be built overnight. If you truly want to become the best that you can become, prepare for a lengthy journey fraught with obstacles and disappointments.

But also prepare for the celebration when you reach the destination. Achieving quality is worth the journey. Just ask those who are already there.

#48

Ten Questions to Ask about Quality

1. How much will it cost to do it right the first time?
2. How much are we losing by not doing it right the first time?
3. What's the difference between 1 and 2?
4. Are we demanding quality from our vendors and suppliers?
5. Are we concealing poor service and product with cosmetic, superficial actions?
6. Is everyone in this company committed to quality?
7. Are we prepared to invest time and money to attain quality?
8. How do we define quality?

9. How do we measure quality?
10. What can we do to ensure that quality is in every employee's best interest?

#49

Eight Principles of Quality Improvement

1. **Quality is defined as the fulfillment of management's expectations.**

   Quality exists when management establishes worthwhile objectives; translates them into expectations for employee behavior; communicates these expectations to properly hired, properly trained employees; motivates employees to meet those expectations; and monitors their fulfillment.

2. **Quality improvement programs do not have to begin with data collection.**

   Formal evaluation of product or service outcomes is expensive, unreliable, and unnecessary for the open-eyed manager. You should already be collecting information from customers on how well you're doing. There's nothing else you need to know. Focus on improving the work process rather than on inspecting, checking, and testing. Roll up your sleeves and straighten things out.

3. **The performance objective in high-quality companies is to be 100% error-free.**

   A company with an acceptable quality standard of 99% is saying to employees, "It's okay for you to screw up 1% of the time." The most fundamental quality objective is DIRFT—"Do It Right the First Time." Consider how unacceptable even a 99.9% quality rate can be. If the U.S. Post Office accepted this quality standard, it would be happy to lose 500,000 pieces of mail each day.

4. **Humans are *not* destined to make mistakes.**

   Errors are a function of the importance managers (and consequently employees) place on the job. Employees who make mistakes expect them to happen and are not upset when they do. The units in your organization where the fewest mistakes are made are led by managers who are least tolerant of mistakes.

5. **The most important quality question is "What is the cost of not doing it right the first time?"**

   Precisely how much time, effort, materials, and money are spent correcting errors made by employees? Low-performing companies never think of compiling this figure.

6. **The second most important quality question is "What investment is needed to *ensure* that work is done right the first time?"**

   Comparing this investment to the cost of not doing it right the first time tells you whether and how vigorously to proceed with quality improvement.

7. **Successful quality improvement programs *do not* focus on employees.**

   Employees who provide customer service or who directly produce products have been recipients of most, if not all, of the training to improve quality. While immediate benefits appear, they are short-lived because of a lack of reinforcement and support from managers.

8. **Successful quality improvement programs focus on managers.**

   Supervisors need to be taught the art of getting people to give their best. It is their responsibility to *empower* employees to produce quality. They provide the foundation for long-term quality performance by providing management that will support, reinforce, and sustain employees' efforts. *Senior* management must also understand this concept and support the quality improvement efforts of supervisors. The management team must be just that—a team. (51)

#50

Ten Key Areas in Which to Strive for Better Quality

1. **Customer service.**
   Improve your employees' attitudes toward customers. Give them reason to feel ownership of your operation and to think "we" rather than "they." Increase their willingness to smile, say hello, and be helpful.

2. **Customer satisfaction.**
   Don't rely merely on market share to determine how well your product or service is doing. Find out what customers think of what you do. Survey their opinions and let them give you ideas on how to improve.

3. **Innovation.**
   Today's hot product or service is tomorrow's buggy whip. The leading companies of tomorrow are researching new markets and new products today.

4. **Productivity.**
   Organizations can be streamlined. Better managers can be hired. Existing employees can learn new skills. Machines can be improved. Systems can be tightened. Lead time can be cut.

5. **Management performance.**
   Middle managers are the heart of any organization. Train them to provide the support and encouragement employees need. Train top management to empower middle managers to carry out their critical task. (106, 107)

6. **Employee performance.**
   Hire eagles, not turkeys. Teach them what they need to know. Support and encourage their efforts. (36–47)

7. **Resource utilization.**
   This does not mean cutting back on expenses to the point where employees have to start buying their own

pens. It means examining and increasing the efficiency with which physical, financial, and human resources are converted into goal achievement.

8. **Planning.**

Generate better strategic plans by systematically involving those who can contribute to their creation. Communicate strategic plans to the people who must make them work. Periodically measure actual results. Consider involving a consultant. Follow these same steps for short-term plans, driven by your strategic plans, in all units of the organization. (111, 112)

9. **Social responsibility.**

It is no longer possible for a company to be indifferent to the welfare of the community, the country, and even the world. Indeed, it is in every organization's self-interest to excel in nonprofit-making benefits to its environment and community.

10. **Bottom line.**

The rationale for focusing on any of these areas is to improve your organization's bottom line—whether that means profit, service, or any other criterion. The route to an improved bottom line begins in the areas of greatest potential improvement for your organization. Identify them, and get working on them.

#51

Ten Steps to Get People to Give Their Best

1. **Guide your efforts by an ambitious, inspiring, and well-conceived vision for your unit.**

Vision means being able to see what your unit will look like tomorrow, and having a plan to get there. Get beyond the day-to-day pressures of your job. Look into the future—one, five, and even ten years down the road. A vision is your mental dress rehearsal for success.

2. **Share your vision and the rationale behind it—your dreams, motivations, and reasons—with employees.**

If subordinates know what your vision is, they'll be able to help you attain it; if not, they'll be confused, helpless, and possibly alienated. Consider these three strategies for sharing your vision.

A. Include employees in the creation of the vision, by involving them in strategic planning.

B. Communicate your vision to them as picturesquely as you can—so they can see it, taste it, and touch it as vividly as you do.

C. Don't tell people what to do, but what your needs are. Let them help you decide how to meet those needs and at the same time figure out your vision from your needs.

3. **Generate expectations for each employee in achieving the vision.**

What must each employee under your responsibility contribute to the total effort? Draw up a specific list for each person.

4. *Hire* **people who are capable of fulfilling your expectations.**

When you need an eagle and you're saddled with a turkey, no amount of training, rewards, cajoling, or intimidation is going to help. Each job has its own particular skill requirements, but two qualities you need to look for in everyone you hire are communication skills and the ability to work with others. (95)

5. **Make your expectations known—*early, clearly, and often.***

The best time to specify your expectations is just before you decide to hire someone. Put them in writing.

This is also the time to discover his or her expectations of the organization and of you as the boss. Be as sure as you can that a job candidate can satisfy your goals. And after you hire, let people know when the expectations change, and why. (71)

6. **Negotiate to get what you want from them.**

   Every manager must ask this question: "How can I get people to *want* to fulfill my expectations?" Simply telling people what to do won't work. Increasingly, people refuse to be ordered around, and when they do something because they are *told* to do it, quality rarely results. (82)

7. **Delegate responsibility that will encourage employees to reach for the top.**

   When you delegate important responsibilities to subordinates you send them a vote of confidence, you challenge them, you increase their sense of importance, and you give them the opportunity to succeed at a higher level. (38)

8. **Listen to them.**

   Listening tells you what employees need; it keeps you from making mistakes with them; it wins their respect; it enables you to negotiate successfully with them; it raises their self-esteem; it minimizes their frustration; it communicates your caring—it's the most assertive communication skill at your disposal. (4, 5)

9. ***Show* them the enthusiasm, initiative, commitment, energy, loyalty, dependability, honesty, thoroughness, caring, and competence you expect them to show you.**

   Example is the most powerful leadership tool at your disposal. Many people in this world are looking for a positive role model; they respond when they find one. If you do one thing as a leader and expect the led to do something else, they will either not do what you ask them to do or they will be upset that they have to do it.

They may not state their resentment to you, but it will show up in the quality of their work.

10. **Give them feedback on how well they're meeting your expectations.**

Each day your goal should be to catch them in the act of doing something right so you can *praise* them, thereby making them feel valuable and valued. Provide expert *criticism* whenever you, instead, catch them in the act of violating your expectations. At least once per quarter—if not every day—tell them what you'd like to see more of, what you'd like to see less of, and what's so good that it should remain the same. (42, 43, 45, 46)

#52

Six Conditions Necessary for Money (or Anything Else) to Motivate Improved Performance

1. **Money must be *important* to employees.**

Earning more of it must be a goal. This is not true of everyone. At least a few people are satisfied with their pay or other sources of income, so money is no motivation for them.

2. **Managers must have a fair *measure* of the quality of employee performance.**

Sales commissions and piecework can be quantified, but not everyone's performance can be evaluated so reliably. For example, how can one determine the effectiveness of a teacher? Student evaluations are highly subjective; classroom observations by the principal are spotty. If a single objective measure were used, such as student performance in subsequent classes, all of the other potential benefits of teaching might be ignored; furthermore, teachers might be encouraged to help students do well on the next term's tests, instead of teaching them to master the present subject. Finding the best way to measure performance requires careful thought and a thorough understanding of the job.

3. **Managers must have the *freedom* to provide employees with compensation according to the quality of their performance.**

   In many organizations this freedom does not exist. Pay increases occur across the board because of company policy, employee wishes, or union demands. One reason employees resist the concept of merit increases is the view that compensation is not a gift, but a right that should not be tampered with.

4. **Employees must believe that compensation increases in *direct response* to their performance.**

   They must be convinced that, "I got this raise because of my hard work. If I continue to excel next pay period, I'll probably get another raise. Therefore, I'll continue to exert myself." Year-end bonuses based on company-wide success have diluted impact on individual effort. Even generous pay increases lose their impact unless the employee feels in control of the process.

5. **Employees must believe that the *amount* of compensation they receive is worth the effort.**

   One of the authors worked for an organization that one year budgeted an amount equal to 7% of its payroll for year-end pay raises—a generous amount by industry-wide standards. Yet top management announced that everyone in the company performing satisfactorily would receive 6%, with the other 1% distributed among meritorious employees. This meant that "top performers" received increases in the range of 7–10%. Few felt that the size of their increase was appropriate for the extra contribution they had made to the organization.

6. **Employees must be *capable* of and *desirous* of exerting the effort that will improve their performance.**

   If an employee has risen to his or her level of incompetence, merit pay alone will not result in better performance. Similarly, an alienated employee may not be interested in working harder, despite financial incentives. Many surveys report that free time may be as attractive to employees as a monetary bonus. Multipaycheck marriages place a premium on time spent together.

#53

Ten Characteristics of a Successful Employee Recognition Program

1. **It is enthusiastically supported by the CEO and other top managers.**

   If not, subordinate managers won't see it in their best interests to make the program work.

2. **It is not tied to compensation for doing the job.**

   Compensation is a *right* that employees are entitled to by virtue of their effort; recognition is a *gift*. Rights and gifts don't mix well.

3. **An organization-wide committee of upbeat managers and previous award winners administers the program.**

   The CEO should acknowledge their efforts as recognizers and rotate membership on the committee regularly to maintain a flow of fresh ideas.

4. **Supervisors are constantly on the lookout for employees to nominate.**

   They have been directed by their managers to spend as much time as possible catching people in the act of doing something right. (This "snooping" process is as important as the recognition program itself.)

5. **Candidates are recommended to the committee in writing by supervisors.**

   Specific accomplishments are noted and documented.

6. **Teams as well as individuals are recognized.**

   Team spirit can be heightened by a competition for excellence between groupings of employees. This approach works especially well when a considerable portion of the organization's work is performed as projects.

7. **The time lag between submission of nominations and announcement of awards is no more than two weeks.**

   Delays weaken the impact of awards, especially those given for specific accomplishments.

8. **Winners are widely publicized, as are the reasons for choosing them.**

   This clearly identifies what managers consider as heroic effort.

9. **The actual recognition or award is delivered in a personal and honest manner.**

   Slickness and over-productions are avoided. Some examples of tasteful methods are lunch with the CEO, a brief ceremony in the workplace, pictures in the company newsletter, acknowledgment at a senior staff or board of directors meeting.

10. **The awards are things that employees value.**

    Ask them for suggestions. Possibilities include: give tickets to prized sporting or cultural events; name a space in a building after a winner; send winners to attractive seminars; give a donation to a charity of the employee's choice; provide free lunch and a special table in the cafeteria or a local restaurant for the employee and coworkers.

#54

Eighteen Inexpensive Ways to Reward Employees

1. A pat on the back.
2. A smile.
3. A simple, sincere thank-you.
4. A personal letter to the employee with copies sent to upper management and to the employee's supervisor.
5. Public recognition in front of peers.
6. Public recognition in front of your boss.
7. A letter of praise from a customer or vendor shared directly with the employee who delivered the service.
8. A letter from a customer or vendor praising an employee, posted on company bulletin board.
9. Listening to an employee who has an idea for improving efficiency and then acting affirmatively on that suggestion.
10. Arranging employee discounts from your vendors or customers.
11. Allowing the employee to work on an especially exciting project that he or she would usually not work on.
12. Asking employees what nonmonetary rewards they would like to have and, if possible, providing them.
13. Issuing a "You Were Mentioned" certificate to employees whenever you hear anything nice about them, whether from a customer, coworker, or superior.
14. Electing a high-achieving employee to a quality circle or to a company-wide task force. (57)
15. Bringing in coffee and donuts after a unit-wide effort.
16. Providing free lunch for employees caught in the act of victory by an appointed group of company-wide "catchers."
17. Rotating the "company flag" or other symbol of excel-

lence from deserving unit to deserving unit on a quarterly basis.

18. Creating a small slush fund meted out to managers of deserving units to do something nice for the units and for employees of particular merit.

#55

Nine Tips for Instilling Pride in Employees

1. *Hire* **people committed to good work.**
   Employees should take pride in good work and pride in themselves. Few organizations invest sufficient resources in the hiring process. (95)
2. **Recognize any employee whose performance enhances the company mission.**
   These employees are company heroes and should be labeled as such. (53, 54)
3. **No job in the company should be perceived as menial.**
   All jobs are important, regardless of what people get paid for performing them. No manager or employee should be allowed to refer to any other employee as "just a . . ." (e.g., "just a secretary" or "just a janitor").
4. **Open channels between the marketplace and employees.**
   All employees should know what their customers are saying and feeling about the company. Share customer feedback with everybody.
5. **Involve employees in decisions that directly affect them.**
   Push decision making as far down the organizational hierarchy as possible. (39)
6. **Anticipate employee grievances.**
   Manage proactively, not reactively.
7. **Reward employees on the basis of group and com-**

pany performance, not just individual performance.

If you can, find rewards that your group will prize. Even informal prizes are pleasing. Take doughnuts in once in a while or order a pizza lunch.

8. **Create task forces and project teams composed of members from different departments.**

Cut across hierarchy and functional departments. Get people involved in solving organizational problems. Replace "they" attitudes with a "we" feeling.

9. **Try to have fun.**

Work should not be penance. Find ways to celebrate the joy of working in the company.

#56

Eleven Characteristics of Winning Corporate Cultures

1. An uncompromising belief that *people* are the most valuable corporate resource.
2. A support of in-house entrepreneurship—rewarding people who help the company achieve its mission.
3. Control based on loyalty and commitment rather than on rules and compliance.
4. Employee commitment to company goals more than to group or personal goals.
5. Top management commitment to instilling pride among all employees.
6. Top management commitment to producing goods or services that have distinctive value.
7. A belief in the importance of rituals, ceremonies, and corporate heroes.
8. An obsession with information—both the good news and bad news.

9. A realization that upward communication is more important than downward communication.
10. Top management support for training and development—a commitment to being smarter than the competition.
11. A philosophy that values risk taking and creativity.

#57
Eight Guidelines for Using Quality Improvement Teams

1. View Quality Improvement Teams (defined on page 15) as *part* of quality improvement, not as the only solution.
2. Don't institute Quality Improvement Teams unless upper management is committed to acting upon their recommendations.
3. Provide members of the teams with training in communication skills, problem-solving skills, and conflict resolution.
4. Implement a pilot program before you commit to a full-scale program.
5. Quality Improvement Teams should not digress into personal issues that are more appropriate for sensitivity training or encounter groups.
6. Membership should be voluntary; members should be rewarded for their contribution.
7. Quality Improvement Teams meet on company time.
8. The leader is usually an employee trained in group leadership skills.

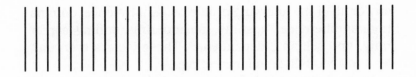

6. Run Effective Meetings

FEW MANAGEMENT tools are viewed with as much disdain as the meeting. Consider these jokes: "A camel is a horse designed by a committee"; "A meeting is a place where people take minutes and waste hours"; "A committee is a group of people who individually can do nothing and who jointly decide that nothing can be done."

Yet to be a member of society is to be a member of groups. From womb to tomb we take part in group activities and meetings. Our churches, synagogues, schools, civic groups, social clubs, and employers all periodically bring us together to achieve goals supposedly too complex for a single individual. Thus, unless you have been raised by wolves or work as a night watchman in a cave, you live and work in a world dominated by groups, committees, councils, boards, and task forces. One recent study shows that meetings increase in frequency and importance as you move up the hierarchy. The average chief executive officer spends nearly 20 hours a week in meetings.

We read in the management literature that meetings are a powerful medium for pooling individual talent and creating a product greater than the sum of its whole. This is the theory. Unfortunately, our personal realities seldom support the theory. We spend a lot of time in meetings, but for many of us this time is wasted. We've probably witnessed any or all of the following problems: ambivalence, domination, indifference, hostility, meandering, stifling conformity, and selfish independence. These factors eventually lead to a total disdain for meetings.

As you'll find in this chapter, we believe that the reality of meetings can live up to the theory. They need not be a waste of your time; indeed, you can look forward to them as an opportunity for a synergistic growth of ideas. However, in order for the reality to support the theory, you must accept one basic premise: a meeting is nothing more than a management tool, and like any tool, a meeting must be used for the correct purpose and in the proper way if it is to achieve the desired result.

When a tool is used *effectively,* it is applied to the right job. You would not use a screwdriver to pound nails, nor a hammer to drive screws. Similarly you should not use a group to achieve goals more appropriate for an individual manager.

When a tool is used *efficiently,* you conserve time and energy. When meetings are run efficiently, you conserve all the resources available to management: time, energy, money, facilities, materials, and human effort.

Study and apply the advice contained in this chapter. You'll learn first-hand why group meetings are one of the most powerful tools available to management.

#58
Twelve Situations that Call for Group Decision Making

1. When creativity is needed.
2. When data for the solution rests within a group.
3. When acceptance of a solution by group members is important.
4. When understanding of a solution by group members is important.

5. When the problem is complex or requires a broad range of knowledge for its solution.

6. When a manager wants subordinates to feel part of a democratic process or wants to build their confidence.

7. When more risk-taking is needed in considering solutions.

8. When group members need to grow in their understanding of each other.

9. When the group as a whole is ultimately responsible for the decision.

10. When the leader wants to get feedback on the validity of her or his ideas and opinions.

11. When sufficient time exists for the group's deliberations.

12. When members enjoy being part of the group.

#59
Fifteen Responsibilities of the Group Leader

1. **Prepare a written agenda.**
   Make sure each member receives it before the meeting. Bring extra copies to the meeting for those who forget them. (60)

2. **Make sure the room is available.**
   Make the room as comfortable and as supportive of the group's mission as possible. Ensure adequate seating, lighting, temperature control, and ventilation.

3. **Provide all the necessary materials.**
   Place as many materials at each seat as is sensible in order to save distribution time later. (19)

4. **Start on time.**
   Reward those who arrive on schedule. (63)

5. **Preview the agenda with the group.**
   Create a clear mental image of the specific outcome

desired on each item so you'll all be working toward the same outcome.

6. **Move through the agenda in the sequence specified.**
   Allocate time commensurate with the relative importance of each agenda item.

7. **Prevent members from digressing.**
   Stick as closely to the agenda as possible.

8. **Don't allow any single member to monopolize the discussion.**
   Seek contributions from everyone; try to draw out reticent members. (65)

9. **Listen carefully to everything.**
   You may be the only one who does! (4, 5)

10. **Monitor nonverbal communication.**
    This will tell you, even more than people's words, how they're feeling about the group's progress. (8)

11. **If you sense members aren't communicating, seek clarification and elaboration.**
    Don't allow confusion and misunderstanding to gain momentum. Help people to be understood, if you have to.

12. **Provide interim summaries.**
    During lengthy discussions, summarize the group's progress to that point.

13. **Control conflict and hostility.**
    Make sure members disagree agreeably. Challenge and debate are healthy—hostility is not. Approach conflict squarely and honestly. (73–76)

14. **Create a climate where all members feel free to communicate openly and honestly.**
    Model the behavior you expect to see in your group members.

15. **Conclude by summarizing what the group accomplished and what the next step will be.**
    Make certain everyone agrees on what was decided and on who has what responsibility for follow-up. (66)

#60

Seven Guidelines for a Good Agenda

1. **Specify the date, place, starting time, and ending time.**
2. **Provide a statement of the overall mission or purpose of the meeting.**
    In no more than two sentences, indicate why the meeting is being held and what it will achieve.
3. **Identify who will be in attendance.**
    Participants should have an indication of who the other group members will be, where they are from, and what they do.
4. **List the topics to be covered, in the sequence they will be covered.**
5. **Identify the approximate time you will devote to each topic.**
    When you allocate time to topics, you establish an explicit weighting of the relative importance of topics.
6. **Identify the premeeting reading or assignment expected of each member.**
7. **Distribute the agenda to each group member at least one week before the meeting.**

#61

Eleven Ways to Get Members to Read Advance Mailings

1. **Mail only what must be read prior to the meeting.**
    Distribute the rest at the meeting.
2. **Summarize long documents.**
    The thicker the reading, the less likely that everyone

MEETING AGENDA

To: Jack, Lisa, Mary, and Luis—Members of Users Group

From : Stan

RE: Agenda for next meeting

Date: January 15

<u>Agenda:</u> Our next meeting will be held February 15th, Room 103, Headquarters Building, 2:00-3:30. Aside from the members of the Users Group, I have also asked Tom Edwards (V.P. Finance) and Mary Scott (V.P. Planning) to attend.

<u>Purpose of meeting:</u> To formulate the criteria we will use in selecting hardware and software vendors.

<u>Topics:</u> We'll go through three steps in meeting our purpose.

1. Brainstorming Criteria (2:00–2:30)
2. Discussing/Evaluating Criteria (2:30–3:15)
3. Selecting the Criteria (3:15–3:30)

<u>Premeeting Preparation:</u> Prior to the meeting, talk to the people in your department. Find out what they're looking for in hardware and software. Bring your results in writing.

will get through it. If people need a synopsis, it's best to give them *yours*.

3. **Make liberal use of space and headlines in the readings.**

Give readers "breathing space" and road signs.

4. **Use double-spaced or one-and-one-half-spaced typing.**

Single-spaced reading tires the eyes quickly.

5. **Limit letters to group members to one page.**

Use appendices to communicate more.

6. **Vary formats, color of paper, typeface, and timing of mailings.**

Consider color coding materials related to specific agenda items.

7. **Personalize correspondence.**

The more "you's" the better.

8. **Flag or highlight essential reading.**

Your readers *are* going to choose what to read and what not to read; help them make the best decisions.

9. **Allow time at the beginning of meetings for individual "review" of documents.**

Do this particularly when you suspect members have not read essential background materials.

10. **Quickly summarize essential documents for members.**

Don't sound condescending or critical when you do this.

11. **Rule as "out of order" comments made by people who have obviously not read supporting documents.**

Explain that the input being made suffers from lack of knowledge from one of the readings. This will encourage people to read if they want to speak.

#62

Ten Ways to Improve Attendance at Meetings

1. Run the most effective and efficient meetings possible. (59)
2. Start and end on time. (63)
3. Give members input into the agenda. (60)
4. Meet at the time and place most convenient to members.
5. Secure an attractive meeting room with good climate control.
6. Serve good food and drink during breaks or for lunch.
7. Control smoking to both nonsmokers' and smokers' satisfaction.
8. Save your most important announcements for the meeting.
9. Publish names of absentees in minutes.
10. Replace consistent absentees.

#63

Eight Ways to Get People to Meetings On Time

1. **Schedule meetings to begin at odd times.**
   A meeting scheduled to run from 10:15–11:00 A.M. will get attention and may encourage more effort to get there on time, especially if previous meetings had been scheduled for a full hour.
2. **Start on time—no matter who's missing.**
   If you don't, you reinforce tardiness.
3. **Close the door when the meeting begins.**
   This will draw greater attention to latecomers.

4. **Put the most important agenda items first.**
   If they are last, members won't see a need to arrive on time.

5. **Items of particular interest to potential latecomers should be at the top of the agenda.**
   The trick is to get them to be prompt because it's in their own self-interest, rather than because *you* want them to.

6. **Solicit help from the secretaries of chronic latecomers.**
   Become friends with them. Ask them what they can do to alter schedules or remind their bosses of the meeting time.

7. **Look to other group members to apply peer pressure.**
   Throw the problem out to the group. Schedule a problem-solving agenda item regarding the improvement of punctuality.

8. **Speak privately to offenders.**
   Tell them of their importance to group process and your interest in doing whatever you can to have them there for more of the meeting. If you are their superior, you may wish to warn them of the consequences of not improving. (45, 46)

#64
Ten Ways to Enliven Group Discussions

1. **Hold morning meetings.**
   Avoid meeting after lunch or at around 4 P.M., when most people experience a significant drop in their blood sugar level.

2. **Serve light lunches if you continue into the afternoon.**

3. **Keep rooms cool and bright.**

4. **Be a facilitating discussion leader, not a dominating one.** (59, 65)

5. **Arrange seating for maximum member-to-member eye contact.**

6. **Have just the right number of chairs needed.**
   Empty chairs create psychological gaps in the group.

7. **Ask questions of quiet members.**

8. **Work names of quiet members into the discussion.**
   This works as a subtle prompt to get them to participate.

9. **Give members more responsibility.**
   Allow them to host alternate meetings, take charge of subcommittees, revise group goals, or even change the name of the group.

10. **Use "virtual discussion groups" to generate debate before the meeting.**
    Create chat rooms on your computer networks where employees can deliberate and debate with one another. These discussions provide a foundation for subsequent face-to-face discourse.

#65

Six Ways to Get Group Members to Make Constructive Comments

1. **As group leader, make your expectations for constructiveness known to the group.**
   You may even want to publish a set of guidelines.

2. **Model constructiveness in your handling of meetings.**
   Maintain a positive approach; don't be overly critical.

3. **Reward constructive behavior.**
   Give out prized assignments to the most constructive members; praise them in public. (43)

4. **Confront conflict squarely.**
   Don't tolerate bickering. Call disagreements the way

you see them. Step in immediately when discussions threaten to get out of hand. (72–76)

5. **Insist upon mutual respect.**

   Group members don't have to like each other, but they do have to treat each other respectfully. You may have to counsel violators before or after meetings, as well as during them. (45, 46)

6. **When engaged in problem solving, encourage members to build on each other's ideas.**

   This is the essence of creative problem solving. Whenever someone offers a suggestion or makes a comment, effective groups will respond in some fashion. Don't permit a series of disassociated statements. The norm in ineffective groups is to say whatever you want, whenever you want, without regard to previous comments. (115)

#66

Seven Ways to Get Members to Follow Through After a Meeting

1. **End meetings with a summary of agreed-upon actions.**

   Specify who is to do what and when.

2. **Establish a norm within the group of "do it the next day."**

3. **Record promises in the minutes of the meeting.**

4. **Send handwritten reminders a few days later.**

   This will tell members that what they agreed to do is important to you.

5. **When action is not forthcoming, call to ask if you can help.**

   This is far more effective than calling to say it is overdue. The offer for help is likely to be turned down, while energizing the other person.

6. **Place on the agenda for each meeting a status report of all actions agreed to at the previous meeting.**

Discuss their progress at the meeting.

7. **Solicit the help of secretaries of members who are delinquent with promised actions.**

Most secretaries want to help make their bosses look good.

#67

Fifteen Ways to Increase Your Value in a Meeting

1. **Get there on time.**

You'll distract the group by coming late. Take work so you can use waiting time profitably.

2. **Sit opposite the leader.**

You'll get more involved and be noticed.

3. **Come prepared.**

Read the agenda; anticipate needs the group will have for data you can bring.

4. **Participate.**

Plan in advance at least one specific contribution. Speak up. Be candid, yet tactful.

5. **Don't monopolize discussions.**

If you feel you have to comment on every issue, you're probably talking too much.

6. **Listen to understand.**

Misunderstanding caused by a lack of listening is the great meeting time-waster.

7. **Speak to be understood.**

Right before you speak, don't be thinking of what you have to say as much as what members have to hear.

8. **Stick to the agenda.**

Don't use the meeting as a platform for your personal agenda. If you ever hear yourself about to say, "Not to change the subject . . . ," bite your lip.

9. **Build on others' ideas.**

   Showboaters won't do this; the boss will recognize and appreciate your value when you do. Don't change the focus prematurely.

10. **Be optimistic about the group.**

    A positive attitude about what the group can accomplish will translate into action.

11. **Challenge the group.**

    Pose "what if" questions. Get members to see their potential.

12. **Criticize ideas, not people.**

    Be harsh on ideas, soft on people. While you're cutting an idea down, lift a person up.

13. **Don't use the group as a substitute for direct discussions with individual members.**

    Don't waste the group's time addressing an issue that can be resolved one-on-one. Don't embarrass anyone needlessly by airing dirty laundry in front of the group.

14. **Step into the chair when needed.**

    Provide leadership at critical points without threatening the formal leader.

15. **Perform promised follow-up.**

    If few people deliver on their promises to accomplish assigned tasks between meetings, you'll stand out by coming through.

#68

Ten Questions to Ask about Your Staff Meetings

You should be able to answer "Yes" to all of these questions.

1. Do members freely voice their opinions and vote their consciences?
2. Are ideas thoroughly examined before being either rejected or accepted?

3. Is good use made of meeting time?

4. Are differences of opinion resolved productively?

5. Do people listen to each other and build on each other's ideas during discussions?

6. Does a climate of trust pervade meetings?

7. Does everyone speak up on every important issue discussed?

8. Do members leave meetings with clear direction on how to proceed regarding decisions made in the meeting?

9. Do confidential discussions remain confidential following meetings?

10. Do you agree with the way meetings are run?

#69

Fifteen Questions to Ask about Your Board

You should be able to answer "No" to all these questions.

1. In working meetings, do members ignore each other's input?

2. During work sessions, do members state their own ideas rather than build on the ideas of others?

3. Are confidential board discussions leaked to non-. board members?

4. Do private communication networks exist between board members and management of the organization?

5. Do members criticize each other privately to other members?

6. Do members criticize each other in the media or other public settings?

7. Do face-to-face criticisms lead to personal attack, defensiveness, name-calling, or arguments?

8. Does the board agree on its role and its use of time?

9. Do members regard themselves as representing particular constituencies, rather than as part of a team?
10. Do members have conflicting goals for the organization?
11. Do members disagree on how meetings should be run?
12. Do members boycott meetings to indicate displeasure with what is going on?
13. When the president asks for a consensus check around the table, do certain members ask to pass, withholding their views until they hear the opinions of others?
14. Do board members differ widely regarding the effectiveness of the management of the organization?
15. Does voting (and disagreement on issues) occur along predictable lines?

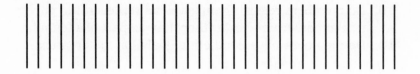

7. Manage Conflict Productively

NAME THE things in life that are inevitable. If you're like most people, you'll probably respond with, "Death and taxes." But that answer would be incomplete. There's one more thing in life that's inevitable—conflict.

There are at least three reasons for the pervasiveness of conflict. First, we live in a world of growing complexity and diversity. There was a time when chocolate, strawberry, and vanilla exhausted the options available at the ice-cream counter. Now you can get 31 flavors, not counting yogurt, non-dairy treats, and other confections for the diet conscious. And for each option we can find someone strenuously advocating the merits of that selection over all others. In short, different people want different things. And very few things satisfy everybody.

Second, regardless of where you work, whether at a large corporate headquarters or a small office, you share something in common with all other employees: you work with people. And to work with people is to experience the inevitability of conflict. Misunderstanding, incompatibility of needs, and bruised egos are just three of a thousand reasons why corporate cohabitation breeds conflict.

Finally, conflict is inevitable because we live and work in a world that imposes limits on our resources. We seldom get exactly what we want; rather, we try to get the best, given the options offered and the constraints imposed. You must distribute merit bonuses among ten subordinates, each of whom deserves at least half of the dollars you've been allocated. You supervise four deliverers, each of whom wants to drive the newest truck. Three of your best employees want to take vacation the same week. In each of these examples, conflict is imposed by limited resources and organizational constraints.

Given the inevitability of conflict, it follows that conflict management is one of a manager's most needed skills. The checklists in this section will help you acquire these skills. We can't guarantee that after reading this chapter you'll develop the wisdom of Solomon. Nevertheless, we can guarantee that you'll see new options for effective mediation of disagreements, and you will get some practical tips on how to survive the interpersonal storms that draw you in.

#70
Eleven Roots of Interpersonal Conflict

1. **Prejudice/bias.**
   Organizational strife is sometimes traced to "personalities." This is one person differing with another based simply on how he or she feels about that person.
2. **Nastiness/stubbornness.**
   Some people go through life with a chip on their shoulder and seem to search for combatants.
3. **Sensitivity/hurt.**
   This occurs when a person, because of low self-esteem, insecurity, or conflict in his or her life, easily feels attacked by criticism or other interpersonal directness.
4. **Differences in perception/values.**
   Most conflict results from the varying ways different people view the world. These incongruent views are

traceable to differences in upbringing, culture, race, experience, education, occupation, socioeconomic class, and other environmental factors.

5. **Differences over facts.**

A fact is a piece of data that can be quantified or an event that can be documented. Arguments over facts typically need not last very long since they are verifiable. But a statement like, "It is a *fact* that you are insensitive to my feelings," is neither documentable or quantifiable, and so is actually a difference in perception.

6. **Differences over goals/priorities.**

An argument about whether a bank should focus more resources on international banking or on community banking is a disagreement over goals. Another example would be whether or not to increase the amount of advanced professional training given to tellers.

7. **Differences over methods.**

Two sides may have similar goals but disagree on how to achieve them. For example, *how* should advanced teller training be conducted?

8. **Competition for scarce resources.**

Two managers might argue over who has the greater need for an assistant, whose budget should be increased more, or how to allocate recently purchased computers.

9. **Competition for supremacy.**

This occurs when one person seeks to outdo or outshine another person. You might see it when two employees compete for a promotion or for comparative power in your organization.

10. **Misunderstanding.**

The majority of what looks like interpersonal conflict is actually communication breakdown. Communication, if not attended to with care, is as likely to fail as to succeed. And when it does, a listener's unwarranted inferences about a speaker's intent often create interpersonal conflict. (1–10)

11. **Unfulfilled expectations.**

Many of the causes listed above contribute to one person not fulfilling the expectations of another. Unfulfilled expectations are the ultimate cause of divorce, firings, and other forms of relational breakdown. The major reason that expectations go unfulfilled is that they are unreasonable, inappropriate, too numerous, or unstated. (71)

#71

Eight Ways to Avoid Conflict Caused by Unfulfilled Expectations

1. **Minimize the number of expectations you place upon others.**
   Hold only expectations essential to the relationship.
2. **Make fewer promises to others.**
   You'll be less likely to disappoint them.

When forging a new relationship or when entering a new phase of an old one:

3. **State your expectations clearly and solicit the same from the other person.**
   In the case of a job interview, you may wish to communicate these in writing.
4. **Test these expectations for acceptability and for appropriateness.**
5. **Negotiate the expectations and establish a contract for mutual behavior.**
6. **Review and renew expectations as the relationship develops.**

7. **Use these expectations as the basis for regular performance feedback in both directions.** (41, 45)

In existing personal relationships, when it's too late to state expectations that should have been stated at the beginning:

8. **At least discuss expectations and ask how well you're doing.**
   In existing work relationships, it's never too late to state expectations.

#72
Ten Tips for Steering Clear of Destructive Conflict

1. **Provide subordinates with clear job descriptions, goals, and policies.**
2. **Spend more time understanding the reasons behind other people's behavior.**
3. **Recognize that rarely is anyone "right."**
   Rather, people view situations through their own unique perceptual filters.
4. **Don't judge, demand, threaten, or moralize.**
5. **Reject punishment as a successful behavior modification strategy.**
6. **Do not accept fighting and bickering in subordinates.**
7. **Take control of the meetings you run.**
   Confront conflict squarely and don't allow it to undermine the group. (59, 73–76)
8. **Search for solutions rather than seeking to place blame.**
9. **Don't let other people push your "angry button."**
   Decide for yourself when anger will serve you well and when you will do better to remain cool. (77)

10. **Work at improving your listening and speaking skills so that you minimize misunderstanding.**

Simple misunderstanding is perhaps the greatest cause of interpersonal conflict. (3, 5, 70)

#73
Nine Steps for Managing Conflict Between Two Antagonists

1. **Listen to both people to understand their feelings, assumptions, and assertions.**

You may wish to do this one-on-one or with both people together. In the former case, be sure the antagonists know that nothing can be held in confidence from the other person.

2. **In a meeting with both antagonists, get each to listen to the other.**

Allow each person to speak only after paraphrasing what the other person has said to the other person's satisfaction. This technique effectively reduces anger.

3. **Point out where you believe they misunderstand one another.**

Don't ascribe any blame to the misunderstanding. Just show it to them. "I don't think you're disagreeing at all on this point. The problem appears to be using different terms to mean the same thing. Let me show you what I mean. . . ."

4. **Check your perceptions of the issues between them.**

Ask questions. Move beyond assertions to the reasons for the assertions. (5)

5. **Ask them if either can suggest a solution that all three of you can live with.**

This is preferable to the solution coming from you.

6. **Decide whether a solution—including one you might recommend—is feasible.**

7. **Select the solution that does the best job of lowering tension and restoring performance.** (74)
8. **Provide any necessary face-saving should one of the antagonists be perceived as the loser.**
   This will enable the solution to proceed more smoothly.
9. **Monitor the success of the chosen solution.**
   If it's not working, find out why, and get the antagonists back together again.

#74
Ten Different Ways to Respond to a Disagreement Between Others

1. **Avoid the disagreement.**
   Don't get dragged into disagreements that are insoluble, not worth confronting, or self-solving. However, don't back away from conflict that must be resolved.
2. **Bring in a third-party mediator or negotiator.**
   This could be a higher-up in the organization or someone both antagonists trust. Such a person might also act as an intermediary between them whenever they cannot communicate sensibly face-to-face.
3. **Remove the condition creating the conflict.**
   It may be an unnecessary rule or some other organizational factor whose elimination will be less costly than the disagreement it's causing.
4. **Smooth over the differences.**
   Get parties to realize that their differences are not that great. Find ways to appease each person and make each less insistent on his or her position.
5. **Focus the parties on a superordinate goal.**
   Point out how a solution will serve their mutual interests. Draw their attention to the common stakes they have in finding an end to the conflict.

6. **Focus the parties on the issues.**
   Get them away from personalities and onto the sub-stance of their disagreement. Concentrate their atten-tion on the needs each of them brings to the table. Often, this confrontation of issues forces an end to a confrontation of personalities.

7. **Point out misunderstandings.**
   Gently show them how unwarranted inferences or lack of clear definition of terms are at the root of their dispute.

8. **Deflate the "fact" myth.**
   Don't allow parties to say, "It is a *fact* that . . .," unless it really is, which is almost never. Expose the impact that their values and prejudices are having on their positions.

9. **Reverse the roles of antagonists.**
   Change the perspectives of the parties by having each assume the position of the other for a specified period of time. A sample instruction might be, "Assume the other person's side for five minutes and describe to me why that person is taking such a stand."

10. **Force them to end the hostilities.**
    Use the power of your position to issue an ultimatum to stop fighting: "If you two can't agree on this matter by 3 P.M., I'll impose a solution that may not benefit either of you."

#75
Ten Guidelines for Resolving Your Disagreement with Another Person

1. **Listen to the other person's assertions.**
   You don't have to accept what's being said, but do *lis-ten* to it. You will learn more about the other person and what it will take to resolve the conflict. Besides,

your antagonist will feel better about you. Paraphrase and summarize occasionally to show interest and to confirm you are listening. (5)

2. **Ask plenty of questions.**

Don't ask confrontational questions, such as those beginning with "How could you. . .?" Ask clarifying questions that help you to understand the other person's position. *Listen* to the answers and ask follow-up questions as needed. Don't accuse the other person of not answering your questions, just keep asking until you get answers.

3. **Don't get angry.**

Remain calm no matter how insensitive the other person may be. Remember that everyone feels justification for their position. Don't waste time and frustrate yourself by thinking, "How could he be so stubborn?!" Accept this person's right to disagree with you. (77, 78)

4. **Communicate your position clearly and thoroughly.**

Let the other person go first; it will put you at an advantage to speak second. As you state your position, look for evidence that you are being listened to and are understood. If the other person isn't listening, ask for the same courtesy you showed. (3)

5. **Focus on issues and behaviors rather than on emotions and personalities.**

Direct attention to what can be observed as opposed to what you surmise or infer. Don't attribute motives; they will simply be denied. Avoid personal affronts; they tend to be vicious, politically harmful, and counterproductive in resolving conflict. The most difficult and most important breakthrough in interpersonal conflict occurs when both sides realize their disagreement is a mutual problem to solve rather than each seeing the other as the problem.

6. **Discuss the present.**

   Don't harp on the past or harbor old resentments. Saying something like, "A statement like that makes me doubt your motives," is better than, "I've never been able to trust you."

7. **Focus on the future.**

   The objective of this confrontation is to create a solution for your future relationship. Hence it is more fruitful to ask, "How can we keep this from happening again?" than, "Why did this happen?"

8. **Take responsibility for your role in the conflict.**

   It takes two people to create and sustain interpersonal conflict. Set an example by making even a small admission of your role, and see if the other person will do the same. A few reciprocal admissions of blame will sometimes end hostilities on the spot.

9. **Summarize the apparent needs and desires of both parties.**

   These are the most important issues to get out on the table, and are the outcome of the first eight steps on this list. You can now focus your negotiations on meeting as many of those needs as possible. Be creative in exploring options and in finding an equitable solution.

10. **Keep the lines of communication open.**

    Plan to meet again soon to monitor how well solutions are working. Agree to talk about problems more openly in the future.

#76
Eleven Steps for Defusing Another Person's Anger

1. **Determine not to get angry yourself.**

   This is difficult to do but absolutely essential if you're

going to calm the other person down. Prepare yourself in advance. (77)

2. **Get on the same physical level as the other person.**

   Both of you should be standing or sitting about six feet apart. When you physically mirror the position and posture of the other person, you help to build rapport.

3. **Shut up!**

   Do not defend yourself or your company—not yet. The person needs to calm down first by saying his or her piece.

4. **Express concern nonverbally.**

   Use your eyes and face to say, "I hear you and I want to help." (8)

5. **Listen to understand.**

   If you are going to present possible solutions, you'll have to know exactly what the person is saying. Listening will also allow the other person to vent and will encourage him or her to trust you. (3, 5)

6. **Speak in a calm voice.**

   Bring screamers down to your emotional level; don't rise to theirs.

7. **Make an empathetic statement.**

   Empathize with the other person's concerns. Say something like, "I can see why you feel that way" or, "If I believed that. . ., I'd probably feel the same way you do." Take care not to be patronizing. Resist the temptation to admit error by your company without the boss's approval, and never be drawn into a criticism of other employees as a way to empathize with an angry customer or colleague.

8. **Ask questions.**

   Smoke out the real problem, which the person may not readily be honest about.

9. **The situation should now be ripe for you to offer a rational solution.**

   Offer a solution that meets your mutual needs as fully as any existing constraints allow.

10. **Don't exceed the bounds of your authority.**

    If you are not able or authorized to resolve this situation, make a referral to someone who can help. However, don't give the other person reason to believe you are passing the buck. Say something like, "Mr. Smith, who is our customer service representative, will want to hear about your situation. Unless you have another question for me, I'll get him on the telephone." Don't ever say, "This isn't my job," or "I can't help you."

11. **When all else fails. . .**

    The techniques above will yield good results whenever you're confronted with honest and spontaneous anger, but it may get you nowhere with a calculating or vindictive individual. In cases where nothing seems to work, fall back on a statement such as, "What do you want me to do?" or, "What will make you happy?" Either of these two statements will often disarm a troublemaker and get to the bottom of a genuine person's concerns. But don't promise what you can't deliver.

#77
Eight Ways to Control Anger in Yourself

1. **Recognize that an angry exchange of words changes few minds.**

   Neither side is listening well enough for this to happen.

2. **Become analytical about the behavior of others.**

   Everyone has what he or she believes is a good reason for behavior that to you looks irrational, childish, or worse. Ask yourself what the other person's justification might be.

3. **Admit that no one can make you angry; you *get* angry.**

    You are the only person who should be in control of your emotions. You injure yourself by relinquishing that control to others.

4. **Recognize that the longer you remain calm and in control, the more likely you are to win.**

    Anger gets in the way of rational thinking and prevents you from seeing opportunities for gain.

5. **Learn to be an observer in your own life.**

    View what happens to you objectively. Evaluate your responses. Determine to do better next time.

6. **Begin *responding* to people; stop *reacting* to them.**

    Think with your brains, not your stomach.

7. **Distance yourself from people who can get your goat and who seem bent on doing it as often as possible.**

8. **When a person earns your rejection, give it.**

    No longer allow this person access to you.

#78
Eight Situations Where an Expression of Anger May Be Appropriate

1. You have objectively sifted through the facts available to you and have analyzed the situation as dispassionately as possible.

2. You have given the other person an opportunity to explain the behavior that has angered you.

3. You have asked enough good questions to be sure you know what's really going on.

4. You have determined not to use harsh personal criti-

cism because a personal rebuke is likely to cause permanent damage to the relationship you will have with this person hereafter.

5. You are confident that the other person needs to see your anger and that it will serve your relationship well.

6. Your anger is directed against an evil or an injustice committed against others who cannot defend themselves, and your ultimate goal is to obtain justice, not revenge.

7. You don't feel personally affronted or harmed.

8. You begin by focusing on your anger—"I'm angry"—rather than on what the other person has done to make you angry.

#79
Eight Ways Managers Can Create Constructive Conflict

1. **Encourage subordinates to disagree and to question the status quo.**
   Reward them when they do.

2. **Hire assistants who don't think the same way you do.**
   But be sure to hire someone who will respect your authority. (100)

3. **Have someone in the group play devil's advocate.**
   Run decision-making meetings so that members feel an obligation to identify all that may be wrong with a favored idea before it receives final acceptance. (64)

4. **When you suspect subordinates are afraid to admit they disagree with you, tell them you'd like to hear it.**

5. **Don't react badly to bad news.**
   On the contrary, make heroes out of employees who keep you informed. (39)

6. **Help your group see challenges coming from the outside that might pull the group together.**

7. **Raise your goals and expectations for subordinates.**

8. **Place subordinates in competition with each other.**
   But don't allow them to sabotage each other.

#80
Twelve Tips for Reducing Your Stress

1. **Practice a relaxation response.**
   Remove all aural distractions. Close your eyes. Imagine yourself in a peaceful setting. Breathe slowly and deeply for twenty minutes.

2. **Learn to laugh at yourself.**
   In a short time you'll look back at your current worries and be amused that you have taken them so seriously. Why not do it *now*?

3. **Put things into perspective.**
   Once a concern reaches the point that it becomes a worry, you are almost certainly picturing the problem as more monumental than it really is. Be realistic! The mistakes you make almost never linger in other people's minds as long as they remain with you.

4. **Take your vacation.**
   You might think you're serving yourself and your company well by working 12-hour days and 52-week years. You're not. You can accomplish a lot more, keep yourself healthier, and reduce stress at home by curing your workaholism.

5. **Cultivate close friends and confidants.**
   Problems and pressures become smaller when you share them with others.

6. **Plan and organize your work more efficiently.**
   (118–125)

7. **Maintain a healthy body.**

   Exercise at least three time a week. Eat a well-balanced diet. Don't skip meals. Get enough rest. Reduce your use of tobacco, caffeine, and alcohol. Have a physical exam at least every other year.

8. **Develop effective assertiveness skills.**

   Learn to say "no" to people who would overburden you. Confront those whose behavior frustrates you. (45, 46)

9. **Assess your priorities.**

   What's really important to you? Do the issues making you frustrated, angry, or sick truly warrant such a response?

10. **Develop interests outside of work.**

    Build a satisfying life away from work. Immerse yourself in a project or hobby at the end of a difficult day or week. Cultivate spiritual values and beliefs.

11. **Stop to smell the roses.**

    Talk to children. Listen to music. Study a painting at the museum. Walk in the surf along an ocean. Watch the monkeys cavorting at the zoo. Enjoy a Marx Brothers movie. Stroll through a bookstore. Spend time at home with *nothing* to do.

12. **Simplify your life.**

    Buy fewer gadgets and household items that require batteries or need to be plugged in. Reduce your social and professional commitments to the bare essentials. Eat and dress more simply. Adopt the attitude that less is more.

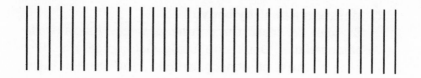

8. Negotiate to Win

FOR MANY managers, the word "negotiation" denotes what attorneys for labor and management accomplish across the bargaining table whenever a labor contract expires. When applied to the typical manager in the typical organization, however, negotiation refers to the process of mediating, arbitrating, and resolving conflicts among the various people and groups a manager confronts on a typical day.

You want to take a vacation in June; your boss wants you to take it in January. You believe one of your subordinates deserves a "Satisfactory" on his performance evaluation; he believes he deserves an "Excellent." The Production Department says the shipment can't get out any earlier than Monday afternoon; the customer will refuse the order unless it is delivered Monday morning. You've got to have a new management information system installed immediately; so does the department down the hall. These and an unlimited number of other examples show that every manager in your organization should have the task of "negotiator" added to his or her job description.

There are at least two reasons why negotiation skills are becoming increasingly important for all managers. First, managing through direction is about as productive and popular today as the mechanical typewriter. It simply won't do anymore. Managers must influence, convince, persuade, and sell—all of which are negotiation skills.

Managers in the era of Ford, Rockefeller, Carnegie, and Mellon didn't have to concern themselves with the "carrot" approach toward influence and persuasion. You did it or else. You could take it or leave it. If you didn't take this order, another customer did. In that era government regulations were minimal, employees were relatively unsophisticated, and competition occurred only within national borders.

But times have changed. The stick is losing out to the carrot. Employees don't want to be ordered, they want to be "empowered." Customers can choose from many more "take it or leave it" offers, from both national and international markets. And the government has imposed regulations that Ford, Rockefeller, Carnegie, and Mellon saw only in their worst nightmares.

Secondly, achieving bottom-line results into the twenty-first century will require managers to achieve more with less. The basic resources for any organization—money, materials, people, facilities, time, and information—will become increasingly valuable and scarce.

Think about your own situation. Compare this year's budget to last year's. Compare the deadlines imposed on projects this year to the deadlines imposed last year. Compare the amount of slack you have this year to the amount you had last year. Chances are that for each of these comparisons you had more in the past than you have in the present . . . and you have more in the present than you will probably have in the future. The days of doing more with more are gone. Your promotability will hinge on your ability to accomplish more with less.

To develop negotiating skills you must first accept the importance of the role and orient yourself toward thinking like a negotiator. The lists contained in this chapter are designed to achieve this objective. When you've studied these checklists and applied them to your job, you'll be able to incorporate the title "Negotiator" into your personal job description.

#81
Eleven Steps Before You Negotiate

1. **Know your goals.**
    Why are you going to negotiate? What specific condition should exist when an agreement is reached? Will you accept less? What is the absolute minimum you will accept?
2. **Know yourself.**
    Can you control your emotions? Are you a good listener? Do you have the patience to hold out for the best deal? Do you have the cunning to uncover all the facts and figures about your opposition? Are you comfortable with face-to-face negotiations? (2)
3. **Know the opposition.**
    What do you know about your opposition's attitudes, behavior, and negotiating style? How rigid are they? What ploys do they use? How confident are they? Spend as much time as you can with your opposition in the hours, days, and weeks leading up to the actual negotiation.
4. **Anticipate the goals of the opposition.**
    What does the opposition want to get out of this negotiation? What is their real purpose in coming to the table? To what extent are these goals consistent with or antithetical to yours?
5. **Anticipate the strategy of the opposition.**
    If you held the opposition's goals, what strategies would you employ? How will you respond to each of those strategies?
6. **Anticipate the issues.**
    What issues or topics do you feel need to be discussed

and agreed upon? What issues might the other party bring up and want to settle before an agreement is reached? How will you respond to these issues?

7. **Consider asking others for assistance.**

   You may want outside help with four aspects of the process.

   A. You might lead a group discussion of people familiar with the opposition to predict their strategies and brainstorm appropriate responses.

   B. You might create a simulation of the negotiation by having someone play the opposition in a role play of the event.

   C. Your self-analysis (see step 2) might reveal a weakness in your negotiation style that you need help to eliminate, possibly through training.

   D. You might benefit from the presence of legal, technical, or negotiating expertise during the actual negotiation.

8. **Plan your strategy and tactics.**

   Enter negotiations with a plan, but be prepared to deviate from it as conditions change. What is your opening position? What will your response be to the several possible positions your opposition may take? How will you respond to a "take it or leave it" attitude? What conditions might lead you to call for a recess?

9. **Analyze your comparative leverage.**

   How much do you need the opposition? How much do they need you? What does either of you know that the other doesn't know? Who is more rushed to get a settlement? Is either party under pressure from the outside? Does either side have a legal advantage? Is one side more motivated to "win" for any reason?

10. **Analyze timing and the physical environment.**

   Can you gain an advantage by scheduling the negotiation for a particular month, week, day, or hour? Is there a particular meeting location that will benefit your position? How should the room be arranged? What materials and equipment should be in the room?

11. **Consider visual aids.**

Positions are often communicated more powerfully with the use of carefully prepared slides, transparencies, flip charts, or posters. If you plan to use these media to communicate, double-check the data, have the visual aids done professionally, use color and oversized images, and know exactly when to use them. (23)

#82
Seven Steps to Sell Your Ideas to Others

1. **Know exactly what it is that you want.**

Visualize it clearly in terms of the other person's behavior or as some other relevant outcome. Consider the total implications and results of this changed behavior or outcome, and make sure this is what you really want.

2. **Be certain you're willing to pay for it.**

You get very little from other people without paying some price for what you get. Can you afford the price you'll probably have to pay in terms of the incentives the other person will need to sustain new behaviors? Are you willing to accept changes in other areas to get what you want in this one?

3. **Ask for it.**

Too many people are either afraid to ask for what they really want, or they assume the other person somehow knows what it is. One of the biggest reasons we don't get what we want is that we never really ask for it.

4. **Be specific.**

Take that picture you created in step 1 and share it completely and in living color with the other person.

Paint bold strokes so he or she knows exactly what you are proposing. Tell the person how he or she will be affected as well as the full implications of complying with your request.

5. **Show the benefits.**

Your idea must meet some self-interest for the other person or it won't be accepted. You need a good answer to the question, "What's in it for me?" Document the specific advantages of your idea. Provide convincing supporting data. Know the other person's values, attitudes, and needs. (5)

6. **Overcome objections.**

No matter how well you carry out the steps above, expect to encounter resistance. The best way to overcome an objection is to defuse it before it is raised. State it yourself as a valid criticism of your idea; then systematically and objectively dismantle it with the potential objector looking on as a spectator, not as a defender. (84)

7. **Thank the person.**

Whether or not you succeed, thank the person for listening to you. If you got what you wanted, include a reassurance that the person will like the results. Leave him or her feeling good about you.

#83
Thirteen Standard Objections to Expect

1. If it ain't broke, don't fix it.
2. It costs too much.
3. It's too risky.
4. We tried this before.
5. We don't have experience with this.
6. That's not our style.
7. Let's wait and see what our competitors do.

8. We don't have the resources just now.

9. We've sunk too much into existing systems.

10. There's too much going on right now.

11. How do I know I can trust you?

12. I just don't think it will work.

13. I agree, but *they* don't.

#84
Ten Steps to Overcome Any Objection

1. **Defuse it before it's raised.**

   The surest way to overcome an objection is to incorporate both the objection and its solution into your presentation. One way to do this is to make your presentation and state the anticipated objection as though it is *yours.* Then dismantle the objection piece by piece. You'll be surprised how many times the potential objector will get into the spirit of the dismantling and will actually help you.

2. **When an unanticipated objection is voiced, listen intently to it.**

   Good presenters who have analyzed their audience rarely encounter unanticipated objections. When you do, be certain you understand both the objection and the motivation behind it. Ask questions if you don't. (5)

3. **Compliment the objector.**

   Acknowledge the wisdom of the objection without being ingratiating or patronizing. "You're right: cost is an important factor in making this decision."

4. **Throw the objection back.**

   Ask for validation or substantiation of the premises or assumptions of the objection. This enables you to assume the offense, not the defense. "Where did you get the data that brought you to that conclusion?"

5. **Remain calm.**

   Don't argue, get angry, or become defensive. Defuse anger with your calmness. Attack the question, not the questioner. (76, 77)

6. **Never show fear.**

   Maintain enthusiasm and conviction (but never cockiness) while answering each objection.

7. **Win a series of small battles in order to win the war.**

   "Well, if you agree that A is true and that B really isn't a problem, do you see that C is also taken care of?"

8. **Answer the objection.**

   Show why your idea is not negated by the objection.

9. **Confirm that you've handled the objection.**

   "Well I think we've taken care of that problem; don't you agree?"

10. **If resistance continues, solicit the objector's plan for overcoming his or her own objection.**

    "How do *you* think we can solve this problem?" If you have followed the previous steps and have not alienated the objector, he or she may be interested in helping you.

#85
Sixteen Steps to Successful Negotiation

1. **Do your homework.**

   Before the negotiations begin, analyze the situation carefully and plan your strategy. (81)

2. **Enter the negotiations with a "win-win" orientation.**

   Winning at the expense of the other party will inevitably return to haunt you. Consistently and persistently communicate the attitude that you can both win from your agreement. Indeed, a truly successful negotiation is one in which *both* parties have their needs met.

3. **Build personal trust and a positive climate.**

   You will get more from someone who feels good about you.

4. **Assume the other party can be trusted.**

   Stay with this assumption until the person's behavior negates it. Trust is the essential factor that distinguishes negotiation from haggling.

5. **Find out whether this person has the authority to make an agreement.**

   You do not want to get into "car dealer" situations where you negotiate an agreement only to discover the other person has to get the OK of a higher-up.

6. ***Know* what you want; *ask* for it; be prepared to *pay* for it.**

   Determine your bottom-line position. Communicate your needs clearly to the other person. Recognize that the other person will want value out of the exchange just as you do. (82)

7. **Focus on needs, not on positions and not on personalities.**

   When you negotiate from a position you tend to lock yourself into that position with the goal of winning, not of meeting mutual needs. Personalities are potentially volatile topics that have nothing to do with negotiations. Don't allow your ego to get in the way. Be as concerned about the other person's needs as you are about your own, and you'll be more likely to have your needs met.

8. **Listen carefully and ask questions.**

   Focus not on *what* they want but on *why* they want it. They may think they want the *what* (e.g., "to be paid at least $56 per unit") when they really care about the *why* (e.g., "to look good to my boss"). (5)

9. **Look for opportunities to match "alternative currencies" with the other's needs.**

   Money is a currency, but sometimes other currencies can have equal or greater value. In the example above, you might be able to dream up something other than a profitable price that might equally meet the need to look good to the boss—it might even meet the need better. "How about if I get appointments for you with the purchasing agents of three other large companies, who happen to be friends of mine?"

10. **Negotiate for the long term, not the short term.**

    You don't want to have to do this again soon.

11. **Don't be afraid to take a break.**

    Calling for a recess is not a sign of weakness. On the contrary, you will almost always return with a stronger hand.

12. **When you arrive at an impasse, bring in new information, set a mutually agreeable deadline, or make a final concession.**

13. **Never make a concession without getting something in return.**

    As you concede something to the other person, you are at that instant in the most powerful negotiating position possible.

14. **Allow the other party to maintain his or her dignity.**

    Provide for face-saving, if necessary. If you have done well in the negotiation, you can afford to be magnanimous.

15. **Establish a clear and specific agreement that leaves no room for reneging.**

    Once negotiations end, you still have the contract to negotiate.

16. **Monitor the agreement following acceptance.**

    If your expectations aren't being met, find out why. Perhaps the agreement needs to be revised, or the other party doesn't really understand it. Give the benefit of the doubt before you jump to what might be an unwarranted conclusion of noncompliance.

#86
Seven Alternative Techniques for Closing a Negotiation

1. **Set a timetable at the beginning of the session.**
   Agree at the beginning that you will arrive at a mutual negotiation within X hours.
2. **Present a "take it or leave it" position.**
   Tell the other party this is it. You've done everything you can—you can do no more. Don't bluff.
3. **Ask the other party what will close the negotiation now.**
   If the other party asks for a specific concession and you can provide it, then you've both won.
4. **Call for a "time-out" and reconvene later.**
   Tell the other party that you're at an impasse and you both need time away from the negotiation. Agree on a specific time to reconvene.
5. **Bring in an objective, third-party mediator.**
   When you and the other party don't know what else to do, call in a third-party mediator. This person can be a mutual acquaintance, a manager in another department, or a professionally trained mediator.
6. **Close with a final concession.**
   End the negotiation by "sweetening the pot." Provide one final concession that will create a mutual agreement.
7. **Establish a conditional close.**
   Agree to live with a conditional agreement for a week or two. You will both try to make it work during that period. At the end of the trial period, you'll come back to "fine-tune" the final agreement.

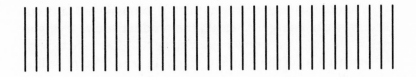

9. Conduct Successful Interviews

JACK SITS nervously, adjusting his tie and tapping his left foot against the hardwood floor. He stares at the clock on the wall and murmurs to himself, "I wish this interview would start. The longer I wait, the more nervous I get."

This scene is played in every major organization in this country on every workday. The only things that change are the names and the nervous mannerisms. One of the authors of this book frequently tells of the first professional interview he ever had—an interview that took place during a formal dinner. At the beginning of the meal, he committed what all waiters and most personnel directors would consider a cardinal sin. He inadvertently placed a scoop of cottage cheese in the ashtray rather than on his relish dish. You may have your own horror story of how you bungled a job interview.

In one sense, nervousness before, during, and after a job interview is totally understandable. After all, this could be the one shot you have of getting into the company—your opportunity to prove that your knowledge, skills, and talents have a market value. Regardless of how good you look on the résumé, if you can't sell yourself to the interviewer, you simply don't get the job.

In another sense, however, such nervousness is a needless waste of energy. After all, the product you're trying to sell is the one you know best. You've had intimate experience with it from the moment you were born. You're selling *yourself*.

Still, regardless of how well you know yourself, regardless of how many interviews you have "under your belt," being interviewed creates anxiety. Not only are you worried about blowing this opportunity to prove yourself, you're also worried about the personal "chemistry" between you and the interviewer. Will you hit it off? Will the interviewer focus on a mannerism that he or she finds annoying?

Our experiences as consultants and trainers convince us that interviewers are as often ill prepared and nervous as interviewees. The assumption that the person interviewing you has been trained in how to interview is precisely that—an assumption.

The lists in this section are written to reduce much of the anxiety associated with interviews. Our tips, based on coaching both interviewers and interviewees, answer many of the "how to" questions you may have worried about.

We've included several lists of prescriptions for those who conduct interviews, whether for purposes of hiring or simply for gathering management information. Before your next interview (as either the interviewer or interviewee), study these lists. You'll feel better about yourself, you'll understand the other party, and you'll be prepared for the task ahead of you. And you'll be pleased with the results.

#87
Six Types of Interviews

1. Informational.
The informational interview is used to collect data to solve a particular problem or to generate knowledge.

Informational interviews are used by managers to investigate the causes of problems, by consultants to determine employee attitudes, by reporters to write stories, and for dozens of other purposes. (96)

2. **Selection.**

The selection interview, also known as the "hiring" or "job" interview, is used to add to what you already know about a candidate from his or her application, résumé, and letters of reference. The higher the position in the hierarchy, the more important the interview becomes. For managerial jobs, it is not unusual to have two or more selection interviews. (90–95)

3. **Appraisal.**

The appraisal interview is typically conducted between a manager and a subordinate after the manager, and possibly the subordinate, complete a performance evaluation form. The goals of the interview are to recognize accomplishments as well as to identify any gaps between desired and actual performance. The interview is also used to make joint plans for the subordinate's improvement. (41, 108)

4. **Reprimand.**

The reprimand interview occurs when an employee's behavior has violated company policy so seriously as to merit a formal, documented meeting. Unlike the appraisal interview, where employee input is necessary, the reprimand interview is one-way communication. The employee is told what behavior needs to be altered and is told the consequences of not doing so. (46, 47)

5. **Counseling.**

The counseling interview is used to help someone deal with a personal problem that is affecting his or her performance. The counseling interview is not mere advice-giving. The effective interviewer knows that most people have the answers bottled up inside of them, and mostly need a chance to talk about their problems.

6. Exit.

This is a special type of informational interview that should be an element of every organization's human resource system. Employees who announce their plans to leave are asked to meet with a human resource specialist who, through a carefully planned battery of questions, elicits their impressions of working conditions in the company. Employees who leave a company on their own tend to be honest with their comments and willing to share information that might improve the lot of their peers.

#88

Thirteen Things to Do Before, During, and After Your Interview for a Job

1. **Research the company and the industry.**

   Get your hands on as much material as you can. If the company is small or privately held, talk to vendors, current employees, past employees, or customers. When your credentials are similar to other candidates', thorough information about the company will set you apart.

2. **Wear your best "dress for success" clothes.**

   Wear the outfit that has generated the most compliments. (126, 127)

3. **Psych yourself up.**

   Engage in mental imaging—see yourself performing well in the interview. Hear the certainty in your voice; see the confidence in your air.

4. **Prepare questions you can ask the interviewer.**

   Questions show you are interested and have done your homework; look for the opportunity to ask them.

5. **Bring along extra copies of your résumé and other documents supporting your talents, skills, and accomplishments.**

   Be certain they look neat and arrange them in an attractive, but not gaudy, folder. (130)

6. **Arrive 15 minutes early.**

   Confirm the time and place. Make sure you know how to get there.

7. **Before you enter the room take three deep breaths—inhale slowly, exhale slowly.**

   When you enter the room, smile and shake the interviewer's hand. (80)

8. **During the interview maintain eye contact and listen intently.**

   Don't start to formulate answers to questions while the interviewer is still talking. It's okay to think for a few seconds at the end of a question before answering it. (5)

9. **Don't answer any questions you don't understand.**

   Seek clarification and examples if necessary.

10. **Answer questions truthfully.**

    You're not doing yourself a favor by lying to get a job. Misrepresentations will return to haunt you. On the other hand, when asked if you have particular experience that you don't have, don't say "No." Say something like, "I'm still looking forward to the opportunity to . . ."

11. **Ask questions incorporating the information you obtained in your research.**

    Your questions show an interest in the company.

12. **At the conclusion, thank the interviewer.**

    You might remark on a specific behavior he or she engaged in that made you feel comfortable. Don't make one up, though—insincerity will be apparent.

13. **Two days later, follow up with a thank-you note.**
    Indicate in the note that you will provide any other in-
    formation the company might need. Personalize the
    message sufficiently so that the interviewer won't
    think it's a form letter. Consider handwriting it. (30)

#89

Twelve Questions to Ask Before Accepting A Job Offer

1. **When people voluntarily leave this company, what reasons do they give?**
   But don't ask the person who is recruiting you if you want the whole truth.
2. **What is the management style of the CEO?**
   Ask almost anyone. You will encounter many reflec-
   tions of it throughout the organization. Accumulate
   all of the data you collect to develop a composite picture.
3. **What are the dominant values of the company?**
   Read its literature carefully. Compare its employee
   benefits to those offered elsewhere in the industry.
   How do competitors view the organization?
4. **What is this company most proud of?**
   Most concerned about?
5. **What sets this company apart from its competitors in this industry?**
   Does this distinctiveness match your special interests?
6. **If all goes well, where can I expect to be three
   years from now? Five years from now?**
   Look at what has happened to other employees as you
   research this question.
7. **What does this company do to reward personal
   achievement?**
   Try to get some specific examples.

8. **How have employees been treated in bad times?**

Is there a reduction in force every time business is off? How are layoffs handled?

9. **What is the personnel flow between this company and its chief competitor?**

Is there a waiting list to get into the company or a waiting list to get out? Is this a stimulating and rewarding place to work?

10. **How much power does your prospective boss wield?**

A boss without clout is a distinct disadvantage to your potential for effectiveness and your potential for promotion.

11. **How valued in the company is the particular work unit I'll be entering?**

Take a look at how well they fare each year in internal resource allocations.

12. **How does this company handle executive management development?**

What are the educational opportunities? Will you be groomed to assume increasing responsibility and authority?

#90

Six Tips for Interviewing People Successfully

1. **Prepare for the interview.**

Determine your exact purpose, anticipate how the interviewee is likely to feel, and create an appropriate setting. Review any background information relating to your purpose. Identify and overcome any prejudices you may be bringing to the interview.

2. **Create a supportive climate.**

Put the interviewee at ease by showing warmth, empathy, and gratitude. Clarify the purpose of the interview and describe how you will proceed. If you record the interview, explain how your notes or tapes will be used. Establish any ground rules. (91)

3. **Ask questions that meet your goals.**

Listen carefully to the answers and observe the interviewee's nonverbal reactions to your questions. Take thorough notes; you'll be glad you did when you later attempt to attribute data to individual interviewees. (92–94)

4. **Answer the interviewee's questions.**

Solicit these at the end of the interview.

5. **Create closure.**

Summarize, check the perceptions of the interviewee, and agree on follow-up.

6. **Perform the agreed-upon follow-up.**

Depending on the type of interview, this may be to send additional information, to report on your findings, or to schedule another interview.

#91

Ten Tips for Setting an Interviewee at Ease

1. Greet the interviewee at your office door.
2. Shake the interviewee's hand.
3. Seat the interviewee in comfortable surroundings, preferably not in front of your desk.
4. Offer the interviewee refreshment.
5. Use the interviewee's first name frequently.
6. Smile.
7. Describe how the interview will be conducted.
8. Disclose something about yourself.
9. Compliment the interviewee.
10. Be a good listener. (5)

#92

Six Types of Interview Questions and When to Use Them

1. **Closed.**

   A closed question is usually answerable with a "yes," "no," or other one-word response. "Do you enjoy being a manager?" Closed questions have the advantage of getting exactly the information you need, but the disadvantage of not getting much depth of information, unless the interviewee chooses to elaborate.

2. **Open-ended—Informational.**

   Open-ended questions are those that cannot be answered simply "yes" or "no." They are designed to solicit a person's knowledge about a topic. "What do you know about our industry?" They work well at the beginning of an interview as they help put the interviewee at ease.

3. **Open-ended—Attitudinal.**

   Open-ended questions are suited for soliciting a person's attitude about a topic. "How do you feel about forced retirement?" They are ideal for learning how a person thinks. You will also find out how well the person's thoughts are organized as well as his or her tendency toward verbosity.

4. **Probe.**

   A probe is a follow-up to a question previously asked. "Why do you feel that way?" The best interviewers make maximum use of probes. They are effective ways to get complete answers and to control the direction of the interview.

5. **Mirror Probe.**

   This is a restatement of an earlier response followed by request for clarification. "You say you think we have a dynamic industry. Why do you feel that way?"

It is often used to check for consistency in the interviewee's answers.

6. **Leading Question.**

   The leading question solicits an intended response from a person. "You do believe that people are an organization's most valuable resource, don't you?" It is sometimes used to persuade, and to let the interviewee know how he or she is *expected* to think. Occasionally, it is used to test whether the interviewee has the courage to disagree, and how the interviewee handles pressure. Unseasoned interviewers should exercise great care in using leading questions.

#93
Eleven Questions You Should Never Ask in a Selection Interview

1. Race or ethnic background.
2. National origin of self, parents, spouse, or relatives.
3. Place of birth.
4. Religious affiliation or practices.
5. Marital status.
6. A woman's maiden name.
7. Existence or number of children.
8. Social clubs.
9. Hobbies.
10. Person to notify in an emergency.
11. Any information you're not really going to use to determine the applicant's ability to do the job.

Consult with your lawyer or local human rights commission. Antidiscrimination laws differ by state.

#94

Eleven Guidelines for Selection Interview Questions

1. **Start out with open, general questions.**

   These will help to relax the interviewee. Make them easy to answer. Before the interview, review the candidate's résumé or application for an item of interest to him or her upon which you can build an ice-breaking question.

2. **Ask direct questions.**

   Don't tell long stories as prefaces. Specify the information you need.

3. **Avoid leading questions or loaded questions.**

   Ask these only if your goal is to put pressure on the interviewee, or if you mean to persuade the person.

4. **Don't ask "what would you do if" questions.**

   Hypothetical questions don't work. They encourage the candidate to guess what response you're looking for rather than elicit an honest reaction. Don't ask, "If an angry customer screams at you about receiving poor service, how would you handle it?" A better approach is: "Did you ever encounter intensely angry customers on your last job? What did you do? Why did you handle the anger that way? What might have happened had you handled it differently?"

5. **Emphasize present behavior over past, recent over distant.**

   Focus your questions on the current job and on its present circumstances.

6. **Probe until you are satisfied.**

   Don't accept mere responses to your questions; be satisfied only by the data you were looking for. Probe until you get it.

7. **Don't bother with questions whose answers can be found on the application or résumé.**

    Read the application and résumé thoroughly both before and after the interview.

8. **Encourage honesty by letting the interviewee know you will be checking information with past supervisors.**

    "I'm going to be checking this out with other people, but I also want to hear your perception of why your job was eliminated."

9. **Do not express value judgments in questions.**

    Never start off a question with "I've always thought . . . ," unless you want to see if the candidate has the guts to disagree with you, or you're simply looking for confirmation of your beliefs.

10. **Avoid asking questions that invade the interviewee's privacy.**

    Be sure to conform with the laws on allowable questions. Consult your personnel office for such laws applicable to the occupational category. (93)

11. **Ask questions that generate information on the specific behavior you are seeking.**

    Ask no other questions.

#95

Sixteen Steps in the Employee Selection Process

1. **Decide which of the following steps to use.**

    The total process outlined below is time-consuming and expensive. Even so, in the case of high-level management hiring, all of these suggestions should be fully implemented.

2. **Examine the job description.**

    Is it still appropriate? Should it be revised before

being used to advertise the position and before being seen by candidates? Get input from supervisors, coworkers, and subordinates.

3. **Determine your specific expectations for the person who will fill that job.**

   These expectations concern the behaviors the applicant will have to demonstrate. They go beyond, often far beyond, the job description. Do you know what they are?

4. **Identify the behavioral qualities necessary.**

   There are often two or three dozen of these unique to each job. They fall into the areas of intellectual characteristics, personal makeup, ability to communicate, interpersonal skills, organizational skills, and motivation. (71)

5. **Identify the credentials required.**

   These encompass education and experience. They're often not as important as the behavioral qualities.

6. **Create an application form that collects as much high quality data as possible on behavioral qualities and credentials.**

   Of course, forms aren't nearly as good at assessing behavioral qualities as they are at capturing self-reported credentials.

7. **Recruit candidates.**

   Advertise the opening, telling as much as you can about necessary credentials and expectations for performance. Be creative at identifying applicant pools. Don't just wait for good candidates to apply. Go out and get them.

8. **Analyze applications and conduct brief telephone interviews to screen for the best candidates.**

   This is the first step in reducing the initial applicant pool to a more manageable number. (9)

9. **Conduct record checks with previous employers.**

   Call only for those you're still interested in. Find out if

the applicants told the truth on their applications and résumés. Again, this will help pare the number of candidates down to a number you feel you can interview.

10. **Design interview questions to collect as much information as possible on the targeted behavioral qualities generated in step 4.**

The questions should measure only the dimensions you have previously identified as important for this job. Don't ask "favorite" questions that have been old standbys for years. (93, 94)

11. **Conduct one or two selection interviews for one to three hours with each candidate.**

Focus on the targeted behavioral qualities and on the candidate's ability to meet your expectations. If you schedule two interviews, concentrate on the behavioral dimensions at the first and the expectations generated in step 3 at the second. Be certain to have candidates bring *their* lists of expectations for you as a boss and for the organization. (71, 92–94)

12. **Introduce candidates to future coworkers for their opinions.**

Seek opinions of strengths and weaknesses of individuals; do not permit coworkers to make comparative evaluations of candidates—that's *your* job.

13. **Call references for additional information, as needed, on the targeted behavioral qualities.**

No matter how skillful your questioning, you won't be able to assess all targeted behavioral qualities in one, or even two, interviews.

14. **Review all the data collected on each candidate to assess the strengths and weaknesses of each.**

When the decision is made by a committee, it is important to begin the discussion by examining each candidate's own independent merits and drawbacks and *not* by voting on candidates or otherwise comparing them. This avoids the tendency for individuals to defend their rankings or their favorite candidate and depoliticizes the process. (114)

15. **Make the selection decision.**

    If you have followed all the steps above that are appropriate to your situation, you now know who is the best available person for your job.

16. **Make an offer.**

    Never make an offer that is refused. Stay in touch with your top candidates regarding their availability. At the final interview, ask, "Will you accept this job if it is offered to you at the advertised salary?"

#96

Eleven Tips for Conducting an Informational Interview

1. **Make certain you are meeting with the best person for the information you seek.**
2. **Reassure the interviewee regarding confidentiality and immunity from reprisal.**
3. **Establish a positive, warm, and relaxed climate.** (91)
4. **Know what you want.**
   Write questions designed to get it.
5. **Remain focused on your purpose.**
   Don't focus on yourself or diversions.
6. **Take notes.**
   Don't rely on your memory.
7. **Use positive reinforcement to sustain the interviewee's cooperation.**
   "That's very helpful."
8. **Ask the interviewee what you might have missed with your questions.**

9. **Ask if the interviewee has any questions of you.**
10. **Honor the time allotment.**
11. **Close with an expression of your gratitude.**

#97

Seventeen Tips on Being Interviewed by the Media

1. **If you work for a large company, refer the caller to the public relations department.**
   You aren't trained in handling the media, but people in PR are. Give them the first opportunity to respond; they may call on you later for assistance.
2. **Prepare a statement.**
   If you have the luxury of time, write a statement and read it verbatim to the media. Don't get caught unawares. Go on the offense, not defense. If you won't be able to read a statement, anticipate key questions and prepare key answers. Formulate a few catchy phrases that present your most important answers in a quotable way. (29, 30)
3. **Make sure the reporter gets your name, position, and organization correctly.**
   Write this information down and hand it to the reporter.
4. **Before the interview begins, ask the reporter how you might help develop his or her "angle."**
   If you can learn the thrust of the interview in advance, you'll be more likely to be able to handle yourself well during questioning.
5. **If you're asked a tough, threatening, or accusatory question, count to five before proceeding.**
   Be prepared with stock evasive phrases. Examples: "Sorry, no comment." "I'm afraid I can't comment at this time." "We will have a full, detailed response

shortly." "We're still looking into the matter." Avoid a confrontation with the reporter. Kill with kindness. (77)

6. **Never make so-called "off-the-record" comments.**
   You may place the reporter in a difficult position, or he or she may choose not to honor the confidence.

7. **When presented with a laundry list of questions, identify the question you are responding to before you answer.**
   If the reporter is interested in the other questions, he or she will follow up.

8. **Don't answer the specifics of a difficult question; respond to its premise.**
   Details may get you in trouble; generalities and premises provide you with an escape route. When asked in an interview if she didn't think that her firm's new product was excessively priced, a corporate vice president responded by saying, "We are striving to market the best widget in the industry and to give the consumer a clear choice in product quality."

9. **Speak in plain English.**
   Jargon or company lingo that may be familiar to you as an insider has no meaning to the general public and may brand you as a bureaucrat. (3)

10. **If you don't know the answer to a question, say so.**
    Offer to find the answer as soon as possible. Then provide the requested information. Don't make up an answer and don't withhold promised information.

11. **If you cannot divulge information, simply state why.**
    Be positive, not defensive. Tell the truth. A half truth is a half lie that will invariably come back to haunt you.

12. **Resist any temptation to criticize others.**
    You are wise not to criticize *anyone* in print or over

the air. You can make every necessary point without doing it at the expense of other organizations or people.

13. **If you expect to be interviewed by the media on a regular basis, get formal training.**

Intelligent handling of the media is a skill that can be learned.

14. **Before you execute a major plan with high visibility, anticipate how you will respond to the media if the plan fails.**

Assume the worst case scenario. What will you say to the media if the plan is a total flop? (110, 111)

15. **Establish a crisis management team or spokesperson.**

Anticipate crises. Have professionals on hand to deal with them.

16. **If the media calls on you unexpectedly to do an exposé, tell them you'll be happy to comply as long as the interview is broadcast live, with your attorney present.**

It looks bad to kick the media out of your office. Conduct the interview but do it on your terms.

17. **Do everything you can during and between interviews to cultivate your friendship with media representatives.**

Perhaps one day when you need a break they'll give it to you.

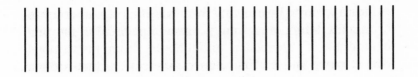

10. Develop Your Organization

FEW OBSERVATIONS of the human condition are as telling as Heraclitus's "The only constant is change." Many of us have already been witnesses to changes in technology, medicine, and the arts which can only be described as astounding. Yet another aspect of our society is changing almost as rapidly and dramatically. Look very closely and you will see something that may have escaped your attention: the companies we work in and the organizations that govern our lives are changing. The companies that employed your parents and grandparents were qualitatively different from the one employing you, which will be different from those that will employ your children and grandchildren.

Certain dimensions of these changes are easily seen. We no longer have organizations dominated by the mindset that management is the exclusive domain of white, Anglo-Saxon, Protestant males. Organizations today reflect the demographic heterogeneity of our country. We no longer have organizations where computer literacy was the exclusive domain of the Electronic Data Processing Department. Today personal computers are everywhere—from the executive suite to the shop floor.

Other dimensions of organizational change are just as dramatic if not as overtly visible. For example, our organizations appear to be evolving from bastions of autocracy to forums for democracy, from jungles of political in-fighting to gardens of discussion and debate, from institutions where power and status reigned supreme to institutions where competence and expertise rule.

Although these changes, both subtle and not so subtle, are occurring within all organizations in our society, the rate of change varies from organization to organization. Some changes are occurring at an agonizingly slow pace. People must retire, the government must intervene, or the market conditions must change dramatically before any movement from the status quo occurs. These organizations will change, but only if they have to. They change re-actively, slowly, grudgingly, and oftentimes too late.

Other organizations, however, take a proactive stance to change. They see change as inevitable and healthy. Rather than attaching reverential qualities to the status quo, these organizations see today as simply one point along a continuum of change. These companies reflect a new phi-losophy: "This is where we are now, not necessarily where we will be or where we ought to be." When these companies change, they change because they see it is in their best in-terest, and they change quickly enough to take advantage of opportunities.

The checklists contained in this chapter are designed for managers who believe that organizational change must be managed and controlled. They believe that even though change is inevitable and that the only constant is change, it need not be traumatic for the organization. They believe that just as money, time, materials, and people can and must be managed, so too must change be managed.

After studying and applying the advice contained in these checklists, you can be assured that not only are you making your organization a better place for you and your colleagues, but you are also making it a better place for the generations of workers following you.

#98

Forty-six Opinions to Measure on an Employee Attitude Survey

Survey your employees to find out how much they agree or disagree with each of these statements. Add others if you wish. Protect employees' confidentiality in order to get honest responses. Take steps to address the concerns uncovered by the survey.

1. I feel dedicated to this company.
2. Ideas for improvement are encouraged.
3. I feel encouraged to learn new skills.
4. My job is challenging, making good use of my talents and skills.
5. I feel I accomplish worthwhile things on my job.
6. My supervisor cares whether I'm happy with my work.
7. People are as important as productivity around here.
8. The standards set by upper management for quantity and quality are appropriate.
9. I am encouraged to assume more responsibility.
10. Incentives exist for improving performance.
11. For the work I am doing my pay is fair.
12. My fringe benefits are satisfactory.
13. The workload is evenly distributed.
14. I am given sufficient time to do good work.
15. My job provides me with opportunities for promotion and advancement.
16. I have received appropriate training to perform my job well.
17. The space in which I have to work is adequate.
18. I have the appropriate equipment with which to do my work.
19. I have sufficient supplies and materials.
20. Temperature, lighting, and ventilation are adequate.

21. I receive an appropriate amount of praise.
22. My work is valued by my superiors.
23. I receive an appropriate amount of criticism.
24. When I receive criticism, it is effectively and sensitively delivered.
25. I get adequate feedback on how well I'm doing.
26. People cooperate with each other around here.
27. I am not afraid to say what I think.
28. I feel free to use my judgment when a decision is needed.
29. Problems in the organization are faced openly and frankly.
30. Important decisions are made without undue delay.
31. The right people are consulted before decisions are made.
32. I am aware of the goals of my unit.
33. My supervisor's expectations are clear to me.
34. Job descriptions and responsibilities are clearly delineated.
35. I get the information I need to do a good job.
36. My supervisor listens to me.
37. My supervisor's dealings with me and with other employees are fair.
38. My supervisor represents my needs well to top management.
39. Top management seems to have its act together.
40. Unrealized opportunities exist for saving time and money in the operation of this unit.
41. I am often asked to do things at the last minute that should be better planned for.
42. The most competent person is promoted when the opportunity arises.
43. It is clear to me what other people in my unit do.
44. The people in my unit care about the quality of their work.
45. Overall, I am pleased with my job.

46. I expect some good things to come out of this survey.

By the way, if you find yourself disagreeing with many of these statements, you're not happy in your current situation. Acknowledge your feelings and take steps that will change them.

#99

Thirteen Questions to Ask about Your Team

You should be able to answer "Yes" to all of these questions.

1. Are the leader's expectations clear to everyone?
2. Are members' expectations for each other well communicated?
3. Are you a cohesive and integrated management *team*?
4. Is everyone working toward the same goals?
5. Do members help each other appropriately, giving feedback on how their behavior affects each other's effectiveness?
6. Are members honest with each other?
7. Does the team have all the skills and abilities it needs to do the job?
8. Are individual responsibilities clearly stated and appropriately differentiated?
9. Is each member doing his or her utmost to help you manage your subordinates successfully?
10. Does the staff communicate well with others, both within and outside the organization?
11. As a group, do you place a high priority on developing subordinates?
12. Does each member involve subordinates in decision making?
13. Are you satisfied as a member of this team?

#100
Fourteen Qualities to Look for in a New Assistant

1. **Loyalty.**

   A successful assistant is one who makes the boss look good. Never hire someone who hasn't demonstrated a willingness—if not a craving—to be loyal.

2. **Willingness to challenge you.**

   You want a loyalist, but not a boot licker. The people to worry about are not those who disagree with you, but those who never tell you when they do. An assistant should keep you out of trouble by telling you when you are about to make a mistake.

3. **Thinks differently than you.**

   William Wrigley, Jr. said, "When two men in business always agree, one of them is unnecessary."

4. **Self-esteem.**

   You want a helper with the guts to stand up to you, the ability to take criticism, the confidence to delegate to subordinates, the courage to make tough decisions in your absence, the backbone to admit to errors, and the fortitude to bring you bad news. (102)

5. **Honesty.**

   You can't expect integrity from a subordinate if you don't display it yourself.

6. **Discretion.**

   You must have an assistant to whom you can speak in confidence. When you interview a candidate, how willing is he or she to spill the beans about former employment? If he or she can't tell you enough, look for a more tight-lipped applicant.

7. **Team player.**

   Your responsibility is to make the team a success. Your immediate subordinate must share your team spirit, and not be out merely for personal gain.

8. **Insists upon quality.**

   Your assistant will be a thorn in your side if he or she does not share your fervor for quality.

9. **Communication skills.**

   You need an assistant who speaks crisply and to the point, makes persuasive oral presentations, writes concise letters and convincing reports, listens to you carefully, and is your ears in the organization.

10. **Substance.**

   The very best assistants always have the data. They base their arguments and proposals on reliable evidence. They maintain good records and documentation, so you don't have to.

11. **Interpersonal skills.**

   Your assistant is your ambassador to the many people you see only occasionally. That person must represent you well by making people feel good. He or she should be free with praise, slow to anger, fair in criticism, gracious in relationships, and knowledgeable of organizational protocol.

12. **Self-critic.**

   You won't be able to give your assistant constant feedback, but you want someone who won't make the same mistake twice. Look for a helper with a knack for self-correction, as opposed to someone who lays the blame elsewhere.

13. **Self-motivator.**

   Your time will be wasted by an assistant who continually looks to you for praise and approval. You need someone who is intrinsically motivated by success. But still praise your assistant as often as you can.

14. **Can take over for you.**

   Most leaders begin to outlive their usefulness after several years in the same position. When you're ready to move on to something else, your assistant should be capable of stepping into your shoes.

#101

Nine Ways to Support Newly Appointed Supervisors

1. **Introduce them to people they need to know.**
   There are important people in and outside the organization who are new to them. Take them around to meet these key people shortly after their appointment.

2. **Give them the information they need.**
   Before their promotion, they were plugged into a different communication network than they need now. They know plenty about the employee grapevine, but little about the management equivalent. Their background in the formal communication network is equally deficient. Spend several hours, if not several days, supplying every new supervisor's files and memory with the information they need to survive.

3. **Legitimize them to their subordinates.**
   In too many organizations people are appointed to their initial management position without any formal announcement. This robs them of the legitimacy they need with subordinates who were their peers. Use the company newsletter, hold meetings, and find other ways to announce promotions.

4. **Advise them how to dress and behave.**
   New supervisors may need advice about professional image. If their dress and behavior are fitting, tell them—they'll be wondering. If you have suggestions, share those too. They'll appreciate the information, especially *before* they assume their new duties. (126, 127)

5. **Show them how a supervisor's outlook must differ from a subordinate's.**
   Followers tend to view their work in concrete and immediate terms, while leaders work in a more abstract environment with a visionary focus. Followers view is-

sues as black or white, while leaders see shades of gray. Followers are committed to the department, while leaders must be committed to the entire organization. Followers work a certain number of hours, while leaders work until problems are solved. Followers care about today, while leaders must be concerned with today, tomorrow, and next year.

6. **Prepare them to deal with former peers.**

   It's a questionable favor to promote a top performer to supervise former coworkers. Peers who applaud the promotion may soon change their reaction to a "Bronx cheer" because the resultant change in work values often makes the new supervisor look like "one of *them.*"

7. **Remind them to keep their expectations in perspective.**

   The high achievers you promote may have little patience for employees with less dedication or ability. They may have difficulty accepting subordinates who are less motivated, who don't catch on quickly, who are slow to adapt, and whose work is slower or poorer. Such employees should strive for the highest possible quality, but recognize that not all subordinates will contribute in the same measure.

8. **Remind them to delegate.**

   New supervisors hesitate to delegate when their unit is in crisis, when the workload mushrooms, or when there is some distasteful task to perform. The immature leader reasons, "If this is to be done right, I'll have to do it myself," or, "I can't ask someone else to do this." Help your subordinate managers lick the insecurity, mistrust, and guilt that inhibit delegation. (38)

9. **Train them how to lead.**

   Never assume that excellent results as a doer will immediately translate into excellent results as a leader. Doing and leading are two distinct responsibilities, requiring different skills and outlooks. (36–47, 107, 108)

#102

Ten Strategies for Increasing Subordinates' Self-esteem

1. **Document their accomplishments so they can't pretend they don't exist.**

   Don't allow self-critical employees to lose sight of their accomplishments and, as a result, lose touch with their potential for success. Demonstrate to them—in writing if necessary—their impact on the organization and on you.

2. **Show them how to find opportunity in adversity.**

   When things go wrong, the human tendency is to despair. But why should we? We cannot change the adversity, so let's find the opportunity that adversity *always* creates. No matter how negative an outcome, it presents options that were not previously available. Besides, when a situation turns completely sour, there's little you can do to make it worse.

3. **Assign them tasks that will display their talents.**

   When you take full advantage of the strongest skills of your immediate subordinates, you increase your own power as well as theirs. By transferring truly important responsibilities to subordinates, you demonstrate your confidence in them, and you give them the chance to succeed at increasingly challenging assignments. (38)

4. **Teach them how to get what they want from other people.**

   Some subordinates are too aggressive with their needs; others are too passive. Tell your best people to reject both self-defeating approaches in favor of *assertiveness*. Teach them the procedure outlined in list 82 for getting others to give them what they want.

5. **Show them the awesome power of listening.**

   Few recognize listening as the assertive management

tool that it is. It is assumed to be a passive activity, when in fact it is an active strategy for increasing personal success. When your subordinates become better listeners and begin reaping the benefits, they will feel better about themselves. (4, 5)

6. **Teach them the advantage of being a sieve over being a sponge.**

   Water passes through a sieve completely; a sponge soaks up all the water it can hold, and when squeezed shoots the water in every direction. "Sieves" are people who become less rattled than "sponges" by adversity. A sieve is less defensive about criticism and can keep a cool head when problems arise. There's nothing wrong with an *occasional* fit of anger or outward sign of frustration, but a leader needs to remain emotionally in control. Help your subordinates to see when they are sponges, so that by knowing the disease they can proceed to a cure. (77, 78)

7. **Tell them exactly what you expect of them and find out what they expect of you.**

   The subordinate you appreciate is meeting your expectations; the subordinate you want to fire is not. Your expectations may be too high, too numerous, inappropriate, or rejected, or you may have hired a turkey when you thought you were getting an eagle. But the reason most subordinates give for why they cannot satisfy their boss is that they don't know what the boss expects. (71)

8. **Criticize their performance, not them.**

   Someone once said that a successful leader knows how to step on people's shoes without messing up their shine. You will have to criticize even the best of your subordinates at times. Do you do it without spoiling their shine? The spirit of criticism should be, "I *hate* what you did, but I *love* you." In other words, reject the deed; accept the doer. (45, 46)

9. **Praise their performance, not them.**

Most people have heard the philosophy of *The One Minute Manager:* catch people in the act of doing something *right.* This philosophy, counter to the prevailing "catch them doing something wrong," positions managers to provide the encouragement, support, and praise that spur subordinates to greater performance. Remember that it is more important to praise the deed than to praise the person. You want people to know what they did right so they can repeat it, and not merely seek to keep you happy. (42, 43)

10. **Send them to training programs.**

This gives them a vote of confidence. If you choose valuable training, you will contribute further to their effectiveness, and ultimately their self-image. (107)

#103

Nine Tips for Managing the Grapevine

1. **Recognize that very few of your employees get all the information they feel they need.**

Anticipate their information needs. Answer questions before they start asking.

2. **Communicate face-to-face whenever possible.**

Written messages or those relayed via a third party may not be understood.

3. **As soon as you hear that major incorrect rumors are circulating, call a meeting.**

Answer questions as truthfully as possible.

4. **Model the communication behavior you expect.**

Don't spread rumors yourself.

5. **When destructive rumors run rampant, establish a well-advertised rumor hotline.**

Make someone available to answer all questions as honestly as possible.

6. **Engage in MBWA—Manage By Wandering Around.**
   Answer questions before they turn into rumors.

7. **Don't try to kill the grapevine—it's futile.**
   It will always exist. Limit yourself to knowing what's on it and to taking appropriate action.

8. **Enlist the support of the most respected group leaders.**
   Send them out to spread the truth.

9. **Have the top managers address significant issues as quickly as possible.**
   Probable rumor topics should be anticipated and defused before they ever become hot grapevine items.

#104
Seven Ways to Promote Ethical Behavior

1. **Model the behavior you expect from subordinates.**
   CEOs who pad their expense accounts are likely to have employees who also break the rules. Don't establish one set of rules for top managers and another, more stringent set for middle managers.

2. **Develop a formal, written code of ethics.**
   Commit time to developing a set of "commandments" which will guide the behavior of all employees.

3. **Punish any and all employees who violate the code of ethics.**
   Sanctions must be imposed on any organizational member who acts illegally or unethically. The reaction must be swift, fair, just, and impartial.

4. **Conduct training sessions on how to cope with potentially unethical situations.**
   All employees should define unethical and illegal the same way. They must also be prepared to deal with "seductive" requests from co-workers, vendors, or customers. Training will achieve these goals.

5. **Listen to employees who have grievances before they become "whistle blowers."**

Make sure the CEO hears about in-house activities before the newspaper does. Establish an open-door policy for any grievance related to unethical activity.

6. **Establish selection and promotion standards that reinforce ethical behavior.**

Select and promote people who are able to produce without violating ethical codes. Establish ethics as one of the standards for promotability.

7. **Establish ethics and morality as an essential ingredient of the corporate culture.**

Talk about it, cite examples of it, incorporate it into employee handbooks, practice it.

#105

Seven Tips on Hiring a Consultant

1. **Check with credible sources to develop a list of candidates.**

Ask your attorney or accountant. Check with the local university. Ask a colleague in the industry who had a similar problem. Find out who does the most writing or speaking for your trade association.

2. **Make sure the consultant has specific expertise in the target area.**

What have the consultants done in the past that directly relates to your problem? What articles or books have they written? What specific training, academic degrees, or certificates have they obtained? What personal experience do they have?

3. **Check references.**

How many clients has the consultant serviced in the past year? What was done for them? How do they feel about the work? What was accomplished as a result?

4. **If you decide to hire a large consulting firm, spend time with the individual or group who will service your account.**

Don't accept any consultant with whom you don't feel comfortable. If the chemistry isn't right, you and the consultant will fight an uphill battle. Don't accept an account representative simply because the firm says you have to.

5. **Ask for a proposal.**

Never hire a consultant without a written agreement specifying objectives and outcomes, procedures and methods, projected length of contract, and costs. Make sure the contract is written in simple language, void of jargon. Know exactly what you are getting, how long it will take to get, what the consultant will do to deliver it, and how much it will cost (including travel costs).

6. **Ask for "best case" and "worst case" scenarios.**

How likely is each scenario? What will the consultant do to prevent the worst case scenario? Know your down-side risk. If the consultant says there is no downside risk, look for another consultant.

7. **Make sure the consultant you hire intends to self-destruct.**

The best consultants see to it that you no longer need them. Their goal is to empower you to become self sufficient, not to remain dependent on them.

#106
Nine Tips for Conducting a Training Needs Analysis

1. **Examine your strategic plan and operating objectives.**

Training should always be linked to organizational strategies and objectives. Determine where you are going before training your people how to get there. (111–113)

2. **Give only such training as is linked to corporate objectives.**

   Don't conduct a training program simply because it's trendy or because you read about it in an airline magazine. Keeping up with the "Corporate Joneses" should never be the reason for investing in training programs.

3. **Check the major complaints you're getting from customers and vendors.**

   What are your people not doing as effectively and efficiently as they could be doing? Complaints are symptoms of training needs.

4. **Examine the major deficiencies highlighted in employee performance appraisals.**

   Look at the trends. What are your managers saying their subordinates are not doing well? Plan training programs that give employees the skills that performance appraisals say they don't have.

5. **Develop a questionnaire and distribute a copy to all functional managers.**

   Ask your managers what training needs they think should be addressed. The questionnaire should be simple and uncomplicated. Ask one or two open-ended questions: "What training programs do you think we should offer which would improve the skills of our employees?"

6. **Examine trends in employee exit interviews.**

   When employees voluntarily leave your organization, ask them what problems they think should be corrected. Problems that can be corrected through training should be so addressed. (96)

7. **Monitor the work force for personal problems or concerns.**

Training programs in many organizations address such concerns as health, stress management, substance abuse, personal finance, retirement planning, and recovering from personal tragedy. Employees will not only feel grateful for a good series of seminars, they will be happier and more efficient.

8. **Administer an employee attitude survey.**

Consult list 98 for questions that will yield important information about the need for employee or management training.

9. **Conduct employee or management interviews.**

This is a more personal approach than paper-and-pencil surveys, allowing you to probe more deeply into training needs. It is preferred when relatively few employees are involved. (96)

#107

Eleven Ways to Increase the Long-Term Impact of Management Training

1. **Integrate training into career progression planning.**

Every employee in your organization should have a career progression plan showing what experience and skill acquisition are prerequisites to job advancement. When recommended training experiences are in the plan, managers can be more confident that training dollars will be well spent.

2. **Conduct a needs analysis.**

Choose topics only after participants have met with their supervisors to determine areas in which they need to develop new skills. Incorporate this information into the training design. (106)

3. **Generate self-development plans.**

   Use assessment forms to get feedback from each employee on which job skills need to be enhanced through training. Incorporate these reports into the training design.

4. **Ensure that trainers use industry- and company-specific language and examples.**

   Many forms of interpersonal, communication, and leadership training are equally applicable to all organizational contexts, but trainees want to feel that what they are hearing is relevant to the "special problems" of their situation. Sensitive trainers recognize this and make their sessions directly relevant even though the concepts being taught are universal.

5. **Provide hands-on learning.**

   If you give trainees the opportunity to apply a new concept when they learn it, they are much more likely to use it. Appropriate application vehicles include exercises, simulations, and role playing.

6. **Provide reinforcement materials.**

   Give participants something to take away from the training session to reinforce the training concept. Common reinforcements include audio tapes, video tapes, and books such as *Smart Moves*.

7. **Favor shorter, periodic training sessions over longer, massed sessions.**

   Many companies whisk their managers away for three to five days of concentrated, and often exhausting, training. For certain topics, such as public speaking, this is the design of choice, because many diverse skills are required to perform a single action and learning is intensely cumulative. Too often, however, this design is selected either for its convenience or to give participants breathing space away from their jobs, without regard to its impact on the learning process. It is often better to conduct shorter sessions with days or even weeks between them. The less that's taught in any given training session, the more that's likely to be remembered. The more time between training sessions, the more opportunity there is to apply session concepts before learning new ones.

8. **Encourage trainees to consult with the trainer privately during the program.**

   Provide trainees with access to trainers during breaks, meals, in the evening, or by telephone. This gives them an opportunity to get professional insights and opinions on the particular challenges they face.

9. **Encourage trainees to commit themselves to new post-training behavior.**

   At the end of a training program, have participants write an action plan they intend to implement back on the job. Have them all meet in three months to share experiences in implementation, or simply mail them a copy of the plan as a gentle reminder to stay with their commitment.

10. **Conduct supervisor-subordinate debriefings.**

    It is often useful for trainees to meet with their supervisors immediately after training to discuss what they learned and how they intend to apply it. A written report may substitute for a face-to-face meeting.

11. **Culminate interpersonal skill training with a team-building session.**

    It's one thing for the members of a team to receive training on how to work together more effectively; it's another for members to apply those skills with each other. A natural capstone to training in communication, interpersonal relations, and leadership is for integrated work teams or staffs to meet concerning the here-and-now issues that may be inhibiting optimal team performance. A consultant should be present for such discussions, which typically occur in a retreat setting for a full day or two. The outcome is a plan of team-building actions to be implemented back on the job.

#108

Fourteen Questions to Ask about Your Company's Performance Review System

You should be able to answer "Yes" to all of these questions.

1. **Does the CEO encourage, support, and insist upon a thoughtfully administered performance review system?**
   When the man or woman at the top doesn't take performance review seriously, neither does anyone else. Enlist the help of your CEO in making performance review a success.

2. **Is there a company policy statement on performance reviews?**
   This provides a focus for support from the CEO. It gives managers the guidelines they need to implement the system. It tells employees their rights and what to expect. It clarifies the role of performance review in the company's human resource system.

3. **Is the system thoroughly explained to employees during orientation?**
   Before they begin working, people should know management's expectations. Explaining the performance review process, giving them a policy statement, and showing the accompanying forms is one way to share these expectations. An even better time to lay out your evaluation system is during the hiring process.

4. **Does performance review occur more frequently than once per year?**

   One review cannot possibly provide meaningful feedback on an entire year of performance. Consider instituting quarterly meetings.

5. **Are managers trained in how to conduct a successful performance review?**

   Don't leave the quality of performance reviews to chance. (131)

6. **Do performance reviews separate evaluation and feedback?**

   Evaluation judges performance so that decisions might be made concerning pay increases, promotions, and other matters of vital interest to employees. *Feedback* tells employees how well they're doing and what they can do to improve. Evaluation tends to threaten employees and put them on the defensive; conversely, feedback will not work when employees feel threatened or defensive. You may not be able to accomplish both purposes with the same form or even during the same meeting.

7. **Do performance review forms minimize reliance on numbers?**

   Rating scales are used on most performance review forms in order to quantify performance. This facilitates making the inevitable comparisons between employees. But employees fixate on the numbers. They tend to ignore the discussions of specific performance dimensions and, instead, concern themselves with whether they are a "4.4" or a "4.5," thereby defeating the performance improvement process.

8. **Do employees have the opportunity to perform a self-evaluation?**

   This prepares them for the performance review meeting by letting them think about their behavior. It is also a good source of upward communication, and it motivates managers to take greater care in the formulation of employee evaluations.

9. **Do performance reviews include recommendations for training?**

Performance reviewers should comment on whether the employee's performance has been improved through recent training experiences, and they should recommend additional training as appropriate. (106, 107)

10. **Do performance reviews provide for two-way communication?**

Employees have the right to comment on management's review of their performance and to note any unresolved disagreement. You might even incorporate a mandatory mediation by a human resource specialist or by upper management whenever significant disagreement exists. Some companies have employees review the supervisory performance of their managers as their own performance is being reviewed.

11. **Do performance review forms focus on the *behavior* of employees?**

Review forms should provide specific examples of employees' accomplishments and failures, and should enable employees to make specific commitments to more productive behavior.

12. **Do managers schedule follow-up meetings after performance reviews?**

The end of every performance review should be a commitment to some new behavior—unless the employee is rated as perfect. To ensure such follow-up, some companies call for another meeting within a specified time period, usually five weeks.

13. **Are the results of performance reviews monitored?**

Human resource specialists or top management

should monitor performance reviews on at least a random basis, looking for adherence to company policy.

14. **Are the results of performance reviews fed back to recruiters?**

    Performance review results on new employees tell recruiters and selectors how well they're doing. Recent performance review results also indicate what behaviors and skills the company values.

#109

Ten Techniques for Dealing with Employee Substance Abuse

1. **Establish a formal company policy.**

   Substance abuse is a fact of life. If your organization currently doesn't have a policy, write one today. Communicate the policy at meetings.

2. **Train supervisors and managers to recognize the symptoms of substance abuse.**

   The major symptoms are: noticeable change in working habits, increased incidents of tardiness and absenteeism, abrasive and irrational behavior with co-workers, slurred speech, lethargy or hyperactivity, and, most important, decreased job performance.

3. **Document, document, document.**

   Create a file on an employee as soon as you suspect a problem. Record all your observations of suspicious behavior. Maintain verbatim notes of related discussions with the employee. You'll need this information when counseling the employee, dealing with a union, or testifying at a hearing.

4. **Intervene only when the employee's performance is affected.**

   Supervisors are experts in their areas of responsibility; they are not professional substance abuse counselors. The only reason for confronting an employee (assuming the employee is not engaging in illegal activity at work) is because the employee's performance has deteriorated. And document, document, document.

5. **Don't play expert or engage in armchair diagnoses.**

Focus on performance-related facts. What did the employee do? When? What were the consequences? Do not moralize or pass judgment; such statements will return to haunt you. Confront the employee with specific examples of performance deficiencies.

6. **Make sure the employee understands the consequences of failing to bring performance up to standards.**

In explicit terms, specify the disciplinary actions you will take if the employee's poor performance is not improved. At the same time, tell the employee exactly what evidence you will require as proof that the problems have been corrected. Communicate that you are willing to help if the employee helps himself or herself.

7. **Remain objective—do not get emotionally involved.**

When you get personally involved in the employee's treatment, you become part of the employee's problem.

8. **Refer the employee to a competent professional.**

Your policy should provide specific professional treatment options: an employee assistance program, Alcoholics Anonymous, hospitals, or other substance abuse treatment centers.

9. **Maintain confidentiality.**

The only parties who should have any knowledge of the situation are the employee, the supervisor, possibly the supervisor's manager, and the treatment staff.

Any manager or personnel clerk who violates this confidentiality must be reprimanded. (103)

10. **If an employee comes to work under the influence of alcohol or drugs, send him or her home in a cab.**
    You could be liable if an employee gets into an accident while driving home. Pay for the cab. It's a cheap insurance policy.

#110

Eight Steps for Terminating a Poor Performer

1. **Avoid making implied promises to employees.**
   Don't promise anything you can't deliver. Many wrongful discharge cases are based on promises which employees say were never fulfilled. Check implied promises in your employee handbooks and the "sales pitch" used by your recruiters. (71)

2. **Bring in a devil's advocate.**
   Ask someone willing to challenge you to discuss the proposed termination, acting as an advocate for the employee. It is better to learn of weaknesses or biases in your case before you confront the employee.

3. **Define your terms.**
   If you are terminating an unacceptable performer, be prepared to define and defend your definition of "unacceptable performer." Make sure this definition is applied equitably across and within departments.

4. **Check with the personnel and legal departments.**
   Be certain you are not breaking the law or denying an employee due process. Adhere to union contracts, if applicable.

5. **Give honest performance appraisals.**
   An unacceptable performer who has been given high

performance appraisals by an unwitting or cowardly manager will not be easily fired. (41)

6. **Document the situation.**

Performance appraisals, coaching and counseling sessions, and reprimands are reasonable warnings that an employee fails to meet performance standards. All such sessions should be documented.

7. **Terminate the employee in a face-to-face session.**

Make sure the employee knows exactly why he or she is being terminated. Let the employee know whether or not you can be used as a reference and what you would tell a prospective employer if asked. Check with the legal department concerning future references. (3)

8. **Make the termination quick and clean.**

Tell the employee on a Friday that his or her services are no longer needed and that this is his or her last day. It's better to pay severance and not have the employee work than to give the employee an equivalent period of advance notice.

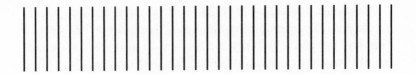

11. Plan and Problem Solve

CERTAIN feats necessarily command our respect, even astonishment: NASA's space missions, the construction of the Panama Canal and the Hoover Dam, Salk's development of the polio vaccine. To consider these feats is to marvel at the potential of the human race. When we closely examine these accomplishments, we find one element they all share. In any successful endeavor, majestic or mundane, success is always driven by *planning.*

Before an explorer, construction engineer, scientist, or project manager begins a project, he or she necessarily asks broad-based strategic questions. Where am I going? What's the best way to get there? What resources will I need to achieve my goals? What obstacles are likely to stand in my way and how can I overcome them?

Unfortunately, our experience tells us that construction engineers, explorers, scientists, and project managers are more likely to ask these strategic questions than the typical American manager. Our work with thousands of managers across myriad companies convinces us that many view planning as a luxury afforded only to scientists and engineers; for operational managers it's futile, a waste of time, or simply impossible.

Although it's not written in their job description, many managers describe themselves as "firefighters." Listen to the way people talk about a typical day at work. "My job is an endless series of deadlines." "It's just one problem after another." "I spent all day putting oil on squeaky wheels." "I can't even get my coat off before the telephone's ringing." Real firefighters work just as hard on fire *prevention.* Protect yourself and your company from going up in flames. Get out from under today's problems to spend time preventing tomorrow's problems and achieving tomorrow's goals.

Another reason we don't find the time to plan is that planning is a future-oriented activity. It forces us to ask questions about what might be or could be as opposed to what was and what is. Planning involves uncertainty and unpredictability. Because the future is unclear, many believe that planning for it is little more than conjecturing—making guesses about the unknown.

A third inhibition to planning is that our society rewards the doers, not the thinkers. We erect statues and name streets after people who successfully execute the plan, not those who devise it. The larger-than-life movie heroes—Clark Gable, Gary Cooper, John Wayne, and Errol Flynn—developed mythical proportions not by thinking about what they would do to the bad guys but by doing it. Because planning does not appear to have the same status in our society as doing, managers are simply following what they believe to be the societal norm. Successfully execute the plan and you'll be the hero; successfully devise it and you'll be forgotten.

Finally, we are poor planners because we simply don't have the requisite skills. We know we should do it, and we know that there probably is a more effective way to plan, but we don't know what that is. We realize that planning is a skill that can be learned; we just haven't learned it yet.

This chapter is based on the premise that firefighters, uncertainty avoiders, doers, and the well-intentioned but misinformed can all benefit from simple, direct, and practical advice on planning. Even if you're averse to planning, you can find something in the following lists to make you sit back and say, "Gee, maybe I ought to try this." This chapter also contains several checklists for problem solvers that will help you evaluate your plans and implement them successfully.

Remember that even though successful ventures are always based on planning, successful planning does not always result in successful ventures. We cannot guarantee that the following lists will make you a success. However, we can guarantee that disregarding the lists will make you fail. Or, in the words of a long-forgotten sage, "those who fail to plan, plan to fail."

#111

Eleven Characteristics of an Effective Plan

These features must all be in place before the plan is implemented.

1. It is stated clearly in terms of the desired end results.
2. It is put into writing.
3. It has been drafted by people who will also be responsible for its implementation.
4. It has been communicated to all those it affects for their comments.
5. One person is ultimately accountable for its implementation.
6. A specific date is established for its completion; earlier dates are established for intermediate milestones as appropriate.

7. Criteria for success of the plan and how to apply those criteria are determined.

8. Intermediate review steps for "go/no go" decisions or revisions of the plan are laced throughout the implementation period.

9. Potential problems that may arise during implementation are identified and anticipated with preventive action.

10. Potential opportunities that may arise during implementation are identified so as to take advantage of them.

11. The supervisor of the plan is held accountable for reporting progress and revisions to the plan on a regular basis to superiors and to all those involved with implementation.

#112
Ten Steps in Forming a Strategic Plan

1. **Determine the motivation for planning.**
   Why are we doing it? Merely to satisfy higher-ups, because it's the "in" thing to do, or because we anticipate specific benefits? What are they?

2. **Establish your corporate or organizational mission.**
   What is our reason for existence? What markets are we trying to serve? What products or services do we provide? Who are our customers or clients? The mission is a general statement providing overall direction for the organization.

3. **Conduct an external environmental assessment.**
   What are the major trends (technological, political,

economic, social) affecting our business? Which trends are threats? Which are opportunities?

4. **Conduct an internal organizational assessment.**
   What do we do extremely well? What do we do poorly? What are our distinctive competencies? What are our distinctive weaknesses?

5. **Establish short-term objectives based on these assessments.**
   What should we be doing immediately to respond to mandated change, to take advantage of external opportunities, and to make desired improvements?

6. **Establish long-term objectives based on your mission.**
   What should we be doing within five years to change the direction of our company so that we are more advantageously positioned? (113)

7. **Arrange the objectives in priority order.**
   You may not have the time or resources to do them all. Work first on the most urgent and on the ones expected to have the greatest positive impact on the mission.

8. **Perform a force-field analysis on each objective.**
   What forces act against accomplishment of the objective? What forces act in its favor? List them all.

9. **Develop plans for achieving each objective.**
   For each objective, *what* actions will minimize the negative forces and maximize the positive forces uncovered in the force-field analysis? *Who* has responsibility for each action? *When* and *where* will it be accomplished? What *resources* will be required? (111)

10. **Revisit the plan quarterly to measure progress.**
    You may discover the need to create new objectives or to abandon inappropriate ones. New action plans may be needed for others.

#113

Ten Characteristics of Effective Goals

1. **Goals should be specific.**
   Not "to improve productivity," but "to return to last year's level of output."
2. **Goals should be quantitative rather than qualitative.**
   Not "to provide better customer service," but "to reduce complaints to 0.25% of customer contacts."
3. **Goals should be challenging yet achievable.**
4. **Individual goals should be linked to group goals.**
   Group goals should ultimately be linked to organizational goals.
5. **Goals should be arrived at participatively.**
   The people who must achieve them should have a hand in setting them.
6. **Goals should reflect critical success factors.**
   Critical success factors are those issues, behaviors, performance standards, resources, and other elements that spell success or failure for a particular company or individual. Goals will, of course, be set in other areas as well, but the critical success factors must take priority. (50)
7. **The total set of goals should be mutually reinforcing.**
   One goal should not have to be achieved at the expense of another.
8. **Goals should focus not only on ends but also on means.**
   Attention to means is especially needed when setting objectives for employees' performance.
9. **Developing oneself and developing subordinates should be part of every manager's set of goals.**
10. **Goals should be written down.**
    If it isn't in writing, it's not a goal. It certainly isn't a *shared* goal.

#114

Fourteen Steps in Analytical Decision Making

1. **Perform a situation analysis.**

   What are the conditions in the area where you are about to make a decision? What trends are good? What trends are bad? Which are still too unclear to call? What exactly is giving rise to the need for a decision?

2. **Determine the decision objective.**

   Why are you making this decision? What do you hope to gain? Complete the sentence, "How to . . .," as in, "How to reduce theft by employees," or "How to choose the best job offer."

3. **Quantify expected results.**

   Visualize the decision already made. What specific new conditions now exist? Are they what you really want? You can't evaluate the quality of decision making without a quantified target. "How to reduce pilferage to 50% below our industry average."

4. **Identify available information.**

   The quality of any decision is directly determined by the quality of information going into that decision. What information can you garner from employees, competitors, experts, files, or publications?

5. **Identify other resources.**

   If your decision requires money, talent, time, equipment, or materials, how much of each is available? Can you generate more if necessary? Where will you look? By when?

6. **Establish decision requirements.**

   What are the conditions that *must* be met by the decision? For example, if you are considering a new job, is there an absolute minimum salary you will accept? Are there locations you would not consider?

7. Determine desirable features.

Decision requirements are the "musts"; desirable features are the "wants." What conditions will be important to gain but are not absolutely essential? For example, you may want a job with no supervisory responsibility, but you wouldn't turn down an otherwise "dream job" that involved supervision of others.

8. Rate desirable features.

Not all wants are of the same importance. Indicate differences by assigning each feature a weight out of a total of 1.0. For instance, "minimal supervisory responsibilities" might be weighted as a 0.3, while "health benefits" might be more important at 0.7.

9. Generate alternatives.

What are all the possible choices available to you? Generate as many alternatives as possible. If you were looking for a new office location, you would brainstorm as many possibilities as you could. Similarly, in hiring a new assistant, you desire to get several qualified applicants to apply, though you might choose to screen candidates so as to limit applications to a manageable number. (117)

10. Test alternatives.

Measure each alternative against your list of requirements. When an alternative fails even one requirement, reject it, unless the alternative or the requirement can be modified.

11. Evaluate alternatives.

Compare desirable features of screened alternatives and give each alternative a comparative rating on each feature. For example, new job possibility A might get a 6 out of 10 on supervisory responsibilities, while new job possibility B gets a 9.

12. Compare alternatives.

Generate a total score for the screened alternatives so that they may be compared objectively according to

REDUCE THEFT BY EMPLOYEES

Program Requirements: 1. $10,000 budget
2. improvement in 3 months
3. production not disrupted
4. no civil rights violations

ALTERNATIVES	REQUIREMENTS $10,000	3 mos.	Production	Rights	RESULT
search employees	yes	yes	?	no	reject
hire undercover workers	yes	yes	yes	yes	OK
rewards for employees	yes	?	yes	yes	OK
training programs	yes	?	?	yes	OK
hidden cameras	no	yes	yes	yes	reject
improve morale	?	?	?	yes	OK

Priorities/Weights: 1. employees won't feel alienated / .5
2. easy to implement / .3
3. low cost / .2

ALTERNATIVES	FEATURES Feelings ×.5	Ease ×.3	Cost ×.2		SCORE
undercover workers	3	2	2	=	2.5
rewards	5	7	5	=	5.6
training	7	4	4	=	5.5
improve morale	8	0	4	=	4.8

your decision criteria. Multiply the rating earned by one alternative for each feature by the weight assigned to that feature in step 8. (The rating of 9 earned by new job possibility B on supervisory responsibilities is multiplied by the weight of 0.3 you gave these responsibilities.) Sum these products for each alternative's total score. Compare the total scores; the alternative receiving the highest score becomes the tentative choice.

13. **Test the tentative choice for consequences.**

Look to the future and answer this question. "If I (we) implement this tentative choice what is likely to happen?" Visualize yourself living with the decision next week, next month, next year, and beyond. What feels good about it and what feels bad? Overall, do you like what you see?

14. **Make your final decision.**

If the tentative choice fared well in the previous step, implement it. If it is not the way you want to go, proceed to the next highest scoring alternative until you find one you like. If you do not see a choice that scores well and wins your confidence, return to step 1 and begin the process again.

#115

Six Steps in Group Problem Solving

1. **Define the problem.**

What are the symptoms and causes of the problem? What harm or dissatisfaction is it causing? What is the gap between where we are now and where we want to be?

2. **Generate alternative solutions.**

What are all the possible ways we can solve this problem? This step benefits from a free flow of ideas, often referred to as "brainstorming." (117)

3. **Establish criteria for choosing a solution.**

   What criteria would a good solution have to meet? What do we mean by a "good solution"? How would it differ from what we have now? What would it look like?

4. **Select a solution.**

   Which of the alternatives that we generated meet the criteria established? For each alternative, have the group first identify positive attributes. When the benefits of the alternative have been exhausted, and only then, focus the group on its negative qualities: What might go wrong with this alternative solution? The alternative that best weathers this scrutiny is your solution.

5. **Plan the implementation.**

   What resources do we need to implement this solution? What are all the things that might go wrong? What are our explicit and implicit assumptions? What is our schedule for implementation? Who is going to do what? (111)

6. **Implement and assess the solution.**

   How well is the implementation proceeding? Are actual results consistent with expected results? If not, what is acting against implementation, and can we overcome it? If not, do we need a new solution? What have we learned?

#116

Six Steps for Determining the Cause of a Problem

1. **State the problem.**

   What is other than it should be? Be specific. Be certain you have identified the actual problem and not merely symptoms or ripple effects. What is *not* the problem?

2. **Measure the deviation.**
   What is the gap between where you are now and where you want to be? Answer this question as quantitatively as you can. How large is the deviation? Where is it occurring? When does it occur?

3. **Describe the factors peculiar to this deviation.**
   What is different about this situation compared to others where the deviation does not exist? What, if anything, has changed recently in this situation?

4. **Brainstorm possible causes.**
   What are all the possible reasons why this deviation occurs? Be creative and even wild in your guesses. Don't judge any guesses until all possibilities have been exhausted. (117)

5. **Test the logic of each possible cause.**
   Given all the data collected, force each possible cause to stand on its own or in combination with others as an explanation of the deviation. Choose the most likely cause(s).

6. **Verify your choice.**
   Validate the cause you've identified by changing the situation to avoid it and determining whether the deviation shrinks or disappears.

#117

Nine Tips for Brainstorming Sessions

1. **Group size and seating should allow for maximum face-to-face interaction.**
   Groups should not have more than 15 participants. Round tables are better than long, narrow ones.

2. **Inform the group that the purpose is to *generate* ideas or solutions, without reference to their merit.**

3. Forbid evaluation of suggestions.

Don't evaluate your own ideas or the ideas of others. The wilder the idea, the better.

4. Encourage group members to listen carefully to others.

Tell them to think of ways to expand, or "hitchhike," on others' ideas. (5)

5. Don't look for the elusive "right" answer.

Just start generating answers. The right answer will eventually emerge.

6. Don't stand on ceremony or formality.

Have people blurt out their ideas without raising their hands.

7. Establish a method for recording the session.

A tape recorder works well. A blackboard or flip chart may slow the flow of ideas, but has the advantage of keeping ideas where people can see them and build on them. If you record the session on a blackboard or flip chart, rotate note takers.

8. Place no time limit on the group.

Unlike a staff meeting, which should be timed, a brainstorming session isn't over until people run out of ideas. Make sure people plan to stay as long as necessary.

9. Use electronic bulletin boards and software designed for group problem solving.

Software now allows brainstorming to be accomplished over computer networks. Check with your software vendor or developer for the latest versions.

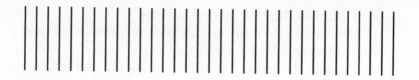

12. Find More Time in Your Day

MOST MANAGEMENT textbooks define resources as all those things you need to get the job done. In management jargon they represent the "inputs" transformed into "outputs" that you bring to the marketplace. Certain examples immediately come to mind. People, money, machines, raw material, and physical facilities are the most obvious. Yet there is another type of resource that we tend to overlook, which is as important as, if not more important than, all the others we've mentioned. That resource is time.

That's right. Time may be the most important resource of all. And the reason is simple. All of your other resources can be replaced, but time cannot. If people quit, you can hire others. If you lose money, you can declare bankruptcy, find new investors, and try again. If you lose a shipment of materials, you can send for a replacement. If your building burns, your insurance will pay for a new one. But if you waste time, it is lost forever and can never be replaced or retrieved.

When we conduct time management seminars we usually begin by asking participants if they agree or disagree with the following statement: "I could get more done if I worked harder." Most managers agree. We then proceed to explain the fallacy of believing that hard work will necessarily result in good work. Hard work results in fatigue; smart work results in productivity. Thus, the goal of improved time management is not to work *harder* but to work *smarter.*

The lists in this section are designed to help you work smarter. When you have completed this section of the book, you will understand the importance of goal setting and planning, how to conserve the time devoted to almost everything you do, how to prevent others from stealing your time, how to control procrastination, and other tips for making sure your day doesn't end before your work does.

Before you begin learning how to work smarter, we want to share with you one more truism regarding time management. You have undoubtedly heard the phrase "saving time," and we'll use it later ourselves. But in a sense this phrase is misleading. Certain resources can be saved and even stockpiled—time cannot. Time is something which inevitably does and inevitably will proceed. Rather than stockpiling it, hoarding it, or keeping it locked in a safe, all we can do is manage how well we actually spend it. In short, we *save* time by *spending* it wisely. That's the first important lesson to learning how to work smarter.

#118
Twelve Ways to Save Time through Planning

1. **Commit yourself to yearly goals for personal development and professional accomplishment.**
   Translate yearly goals into monthly goals and into "To Do" lists that are revised weekly and daily. (112)
2. **Spend 20 minutes at the beginning of each week and 10 minutes at the beginning of each day planning your "To Dos."**
   Ask yourself, "What will I accomplish this week/day?"

Place these objectives into three categories—A, B, and C—according to their value to you. Work on the A's. Resist the temptation to get easier work out of the way first. Turn to the B's next. Consider doing away with or cutting back on the attention given to C's.

3. **Buy or construct your own comprehensive calendar planning system.**

   It will help you follow the three preceding suggestions. Carry it everywhere you go. Use it as a reminder of your commitments and as a diary of your activities.

4. **Create a time analysis chart of your activities.**

   Break your day into 15-minute blocks. Note your chief activities for each block. After logging your activities for a week or so, you'll have a representative sample of how your time is spent. Study the results. Decide what you will do to make better use of your time.

5. **Do one thing at a time.**

   It takes time to start and stop work on each activity. Stay with a task until it's completed. Besides, quality usually suffers when we undertake several tasks at the same time. What chance for success would you give to a fullback smashing into the line with a football under each arm?

6. **Don't open unimportant mail.**

   At least 25% of the mail you receive can safely be thrown away without opening it. Get your secretary to help.

7. **Handle each piece of paper only once—never more than twice.**

   Don't set anything aside without taking some action.

8. **Remember the 80/20 rule.**

   You get 80% of your results with 20% of your effort. Spend most of your time on that 20%.

9. **Carry a 3 × 5 card with you.**

   On it note everything that happens during the day that you want to remember. Mark down every commitment you make and every event you'll need to recall.

10. **Carry work or reading material with you everywhere.**

    Be productive when others keep you waiting or when you're stuck in traffic.

11. **Set goals with employees so they can function in your absence.**

    Don't waste their time either. (113)

12. **End the day by listing all of tomorrow's important tasks.**

    In the morning incorporate these tasks into your "To Do" list.

#119
Thirteen Protections from Interruptions

1. **Put a sign on your door to ward off visitors when you need quiet time.**

   But be sure subordinates know when you will be available. And take the sign down when you're free.

2. **Establish a time limit for each conversation.**

   Look at your watch when the deadline nears. End the conversation when it arrives.

3. **Meet unwanted visitors outside your office and talk there.**

4. **Sit in front of a sun-drenched window.**

   Visitors to your office won't stay around very long.

5. **Cover the chairs in your office with papers.**

   This makes you look busy, and it keeps visitors standing, not comfortably sitting in your chairs.

6. **Remove extra chairs from your office.**

7. **To keep a meeting short, stand up and gradually move the person toward the door.**

8. **Do not contribute to a conversation that is not going anywhere.**

9. **Rearrange your desk so that your natural line of sight is not out your office door.**
Your concentration won't be distracted by passersby who would also be tempted to come in to chat.

10. **If you don't have a minute and someone asks for one, say no.**
Actually, you can say no very effectively by saying, "Yes. . . at 3:30; come back then. And you'll probably need *five* minutes, so I'll set that much time aside."

11. **Start scheduling 15-, 30-, and 45-minute meetings.**
Most one-hour meetings last that long because the participants expect them to and so fill the allotted time.

12. **Assign certain times of the day to certain tasks.**
For example, use the early morning hours for tasks that should not be interrupted by the telephone calls you know will commence at 9 A.M.

13. **When all else fails, find a hideout.**
Do your routine work in a carrel of the company library or in a vacant office on another floor. Tell only those who need to know where you are.

#120
Nine Ways to Spend Less Time on the Phone

1. **Outline topics before calling.**
Begin the conversation by describing your outline; stick to the items on it. (9)

2. **Precede detailed conversations with hard copy.**
Relevant reports and letters should be studied before the phone call. Fax machines allow for concurrent transmission of hard copy.

3. **Tell chatty callers what your time limit is for the conversation.**
Remind them when the time is about to expire.

4. **Get through the social small talk as quickly as possible.**
   Get down to business.
5. **Stand up while you're talking.**
   You'll be surprised how well this works.
6. **Keep the conversation on track.**
   If the caller digresses, ask a question that forces a substantive response related to the essence of the discussion.
7. **Bring calls to a prompt close after completing your business.**
   If the call achieves your purpose quicker than anticipated, resist the temptation to fill the remaining time with chatter.
8. **If necessary, hang up.**
   End while you are talking loudly, firmly, and with a pleasant "thanks for calling."
9. **Delegate others to make, answer, or return telephone calls for you.**
   The danger in doing this is that the person hoping to hear your voice may be disappointed or insulted. Delegate telephone calls selectively and *only* when you have little choice. (9, 38)

#121
Nine Ways to Spend Less Time Writing

1. **Write less; phone more.**
2. **Learn how to type at least 50 words per minute.**
   Type your own rough drafts on a word processor, then let your secretary format them.
3. **Clear your desk of distracting materials.**
4. **Write during your high-energy time of the day.**
5. **Think before you compose.**
6. **Don't overdo revisions in the name of perfection.**

7. Write answers in the margins of letters you receive and mail the original back to the sender.
8. Give yourself a brief exercise or refreshment break every hour or so.
9. Delegate more of your writing tasks to capable subordinates. (38)

#122
Eleven Ways to Spend Less Time in Meetings

1. **Discourage and discontinue unnecessary meetings.**
2. **Always prepare an agenda.**
   Distribute it in advance; have extra copies at the meeting. (60)
3. **Set a time limit.**
   Begin and end at the scheduled time.
4. **Invite only those whose attendance is needed.**
   Get out of meetings when you're not needed.
5. **Put less comfortable chairs in the meeting room.**
6. **Begin the meeting by stating in specific, concrete terms the outcomes expected.**
   Don't permit digressions from these outcomes. (59)
7. **Be prepared for the meeting; motivate others to do likewise.**
8. **Get down to business.**
   Minimize ice-breaking small talk.
9. **Keep the discussion moving and on track.**
   Make members resolve questions on the table before digressing to other topics. Encourage members to build on each other's ideas.
10. **For long sessions take a ten-minute break after every 90 minutes.**
    The time saved by not taking breaks is lost in reduced attention span and lowered productivity.

11. **Use computer networks to cut back on the time needed for face-to-face discussions.**
Create the opportunity for e-mail input and online discussions. Reserve "face time" for the more important issues.

#123
Six Ways to Spend Less Time Reading

1. **Take a speed reading course.**
2. **Tell your subordinates to write one-page memos.**
Provide an example of the format you want.
3. **Scan lengthy reports for major headings, topic sentences, and the concluding paragraph.**
4. **Subscribe to services that provide executive briefs and abstracts.**
5. **Eliminate distractions when reading.**
6. **Buy condensed books on tape.**

#124
Fourteen Ways to Become More Efficient

1. **Stop wasting the first hour of your workday.**
That first cup of coffee, reading the newspaper, and socializing are the three deadliest opening exercises of American business.
2. **Get enough rest, exercise, and nutrition.**
Maintain your health and build your stamina.
3. **Recognize when your peak energy occurs during the day.**
Allocate the most difficult projects to that period.
4. **When you recognize that your energy level is dropping, take a break.**
Expect this to occur nearly every day around 4 P.M. when your blood-sugar level drops. Walk away with-

out feeling guilty; come back refreshed fifteen minutes later.

5. **Set aside personal time during the day.**
   Don't work during lunch.

6. **Delegate tasks whenever possible.**
   Get subordinates involved in your most draining work. (38)

7. **Work from "To Do" lists.**
   Cross off items as you complete them. (118)

8. **Periodically focus on your long-term vision.**
   If you concentrate only on putting out daily fires, too much of your energy will be consumed by the present.

9. **Take vacations, and leave your work at home.**
   The harder you work, the longer your vacations should be. Four days here and a long weekend there won't recharge your batteries if you work at high energy levels for sustained periods.

10. **Stop smoking.**
    The average smoker spends several hours per week buying cigarettes, hunting for them, offering them to others, lighting up, flicking ashes, smoking without doing anything else, snuffing them out, and emptying ashtrays.

11. **Stop losing things.**
    You may be able to save hours each month by determining to keep better track of personal items commonly misplaced such as pens, keys, calculators, and eyeglasses.

12. **Use scheduling and communication software.**
    Gain greater control over your calendar. Compose, retrieve, and send messages more quickly.

13. **Throughout the day ask yourself, "What's the best use of my time right now?"**
    As the day grows short, focus on those tasks you can least afford to leave undone. Do this even when you're engrossed in the moment.

14. **When possible, plan your work so that your tasks end when your day does.**

Take work home as an exception, not a rule. Your company needs a whole person with a satisfying home life. These days more and more firms are shying away from the workaholic.

#125
Eight Ideas for Preventing Procrastination

1. **Make your deadline public.**
   Tell people when you will complete the project.
2. **Intersperse unpleasant tasks with pleasant ones.**
   Vary the tasks throughout the day.
3. **Reward yourself for doing something you don't want to do.**
   For example, determine to take a day off—calling in sick if you have to—when you finally complete a tough project.
4. **Focus on your self-interest in the completed task.**
   What will you gain from getting it done? If nothing else, your worry list will be one item shorter.
5. **Don't worry about finishing the job.**
   First, get it started.
6. **Do your toughest jobs when you have the most energy.**
   Don't do fun things during your productive periods.
7. **Allocate specific times to the tasks you might put off.**
   For example, dedicate 1:00–2:00 P.M. every afternoon, without fail, to work on that report you've been avoiding.
8. **Don't worry or feel guilty about not doing it.**
   Stop worrying and start doing it. Take what you learned from reading this book and do it *now*.

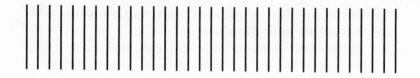

13. Achieve Personal Success

YOU MAY have learned about your individual personality profile from a test taken as part of screening for a job or as an assessment for possible promotion. Are you self-motivated, or do you require motivation from others? Do you like to work on ambiguous, unstructured tasks or on more clearly defined ones? Do you like working alone, or do you prefer working with people? Do you enjoy working with detailed, tactical issues or with broad, strategic issues? These are just a few of the preferences that personality tests are designed to profile.

Psychologists tell us that there is another question that provides significant personal insight for managers: do you believe you have control over your own fate and can shape your destiny, or do you believe you are at the mercy of external forces?

People who believe that they can shape their destiny take a proactive approach to their careers. They believe that just as a company project can be planned, organized, and controlled, so can their careers. If you think you control your career, you approach it the same way you would approach any management problem. You analyze it, establish goals, develop plans, implement plans, and assess performance relative to goals.

People who believe they don't control their careers or are

at the mercy of external forces take a reactive approach to their professional development. They don't engage in career planning, which they see as a useless activity. They believe that what will be, will be, and any attempt to change is an exercise in futility. These are the people who later in life look back on their careers and lament, "If only I had. . ."

The lists in this section are based on the premise that you *can* plan for upward mobility and career success. There are steps you can take to increase the probability that your personal career objectives will be realized. Notice we said "probability," not guarantee. No one can guarantee that you will achieve your goals. Reaching for "the gold" won't guarantee that you'll get it, but it will guarantee that you're at least in the race.

Each of the following lists will help you to enhance your personal image, to improve your style, and, most important, to increase your impact on others. The ideas in this chapter provide you with the necessary polish to excel in your management responsibilities and to stand out among your peers.

#126
Thirteen Components of a Positive First Impression

1. **Dress well and to the other person's expectations.**
   Wear what the other person will consider appropriate for the situation. (127)
2. **Smile upon seeing the person.**
   Let the smile be turned on just for the person.
3. **Establish and maintain eye contact.**
   Look at the person, not down or away, while either of you is speaking. Do not stare, however.

4. **Be the first to say hello and extend your hand.**
   Give a firm handshake—not weak and not bone-crushing.

5. **Deliver a sincere greeting.**
   Consider an alternative to the traditional, and often insincere, "How are you?" Try, "It's good to see you."

6. **Use the other person's name.**
   Say it firmly and positively. Be certain you pronounce it correctly. (128)

7. **Don't speak too quietly or too loudly.**
   Speaking in hushed tones may be interpreted as a sign of insecurity. On the other hand, some people equate loudness with rudeness.

8. **If you are the host, make expected offers of hospitality, such as coffee and cold drinks.**
   If your guest is from another culture, find out in advance what the hospitality expectations will be.

9. **If the meeting is in your office, greet the person at your door.**
   Better yet, meet the person outside your office and escort him or her to your office.

10. **If you are the guest, take cues from your host and others.**
    Observe local customs.

11. **Do your homework about the person and about his or her company.**
    Work your knowledge of the person into the conversation.

12. **Observe basic rules of politeness and etiquette.**
    Especially, don't interrupt the person. Invest in one of the modern books of business etiquette if you feel unsure.

13. **Do more listening than talking!**
    You'll be seen as intelligent, respectful, and caring. However, if the other person is a good listener, and wants *you* to talk, oblige him or her. (5)

#127

Twelve Tips on Personal Appearance

1. **Use as a role model a successful person above you in the hierarchy.**
   Dress for the job you want to have.
2. **Stay away from trendy fashions.**
   Purchase today for tomorrow.
3. **Choose fabrics that look good and will last.**
   Choose jewelry and accessories that are subdued, understated.
5. **Look at your total image in the mirror.**
   Do this at least three times a day: at the start of the day, the middle of the day, the end of the day.
6. **Coordinate colors, fabrics, and shoes.**
   Seek the advice of a professional clothier.
7. **Look at what other people are wearing.**
   Make a mental note of clothing "looks" that might work for you and those that probably won't.
8. **Clean your clothes and shoes on a regular basis.**
   You'll be surprised to know how many people make profound judgments about others according to the style and care of their shoes.
9. **Buy a good guidebook on dress and style.**
   Choose one appropriate to your profession and your career goals.
10. **Maintain personal hygiene.**
    Be totally secure in the fact that you are clean, look clean, and smell clean.
11. **Be attentive to what other people say about your appearance.**
    Seek objective feedback from a trusted colleague.
12. **If your boss or client is going to ride in your car, make sure it's clean.**

#128

Six Steps for Remembering a Person's Name

1. **Look at the person's face for an unusual feature.**
   The idea is for your eyes to be drawn to this feature the next time you look at the person. Some typical memorable features are: moles, scars, size and structure of noses, wrinkles or creases, and lip shapes.

2. **As the person is introduced to you, listen to the name.**
   Pay more attention to it than to anything else being said. (5)

3. **Immediately translate the person's name into an object with a vivid mental image.**
   For example, Paul may become a ball and Karla may become a car. (It will be useful to prepare standard translations for many of the names you can expect to encounter.)

4. **Repeat the person's full name as you acknowledge the introduction.**
   "Hello, Karla Hutton." Don't feel obliged to utter, "It's nice to meet you." Such phrases just get in the way of concentrating on the person's name.

5. **As you repeat the name, use your imagination to physically associate the object with the distinguishing facial feature.**
   The more absurd, animated, vivid, and even violent the association, the more likely you will see the object—and recall the name—the next time you look at the face.

6. **Following the encounter, look back at the person a few times to reinforce the association you made with his or her face.**
   This reinforcement will increase your powers of recollection. The more often you do it, the more entrenched your mental image becomes, and the harder it will be to forget that person's name.

#129

Eleven Questions to Ask about Your Promotability

1. **How was your last written performance appraisal?**
   Do your accomplishments get documented? Do you have a file that will impress a search committee or superior.

2. **Does your boss take you or your data to meetings?**
   Do you get shown off to others in the company, or does your boss keep you under wraps? If your boss always represents your work and never lets you speak for it, this may signal a lack of confidence in you.

3. **How is your boss's self-esteem?**
   Are competent assistants dreaded or prized? Can he or she recommend you to higher management without fear?

4. **Does your boss trust you?**
   Employees whose work is constantly checked by superiors—for whatever reason—are not usually at the top of the promotion list. If you work fairly independently or are given a great deal of discretion in decision making, that's a good sign of esteem.

5. **Is your replacement in the wings?**
   It may not be fair, but promotions are sometimes withheld because there is no capable person to take over the rising star's position. Surround yourself with competent subordinates. (37, 100)

6. **How many years have you been in your current position?**
   If your experience is below average for your type of position in the company, you may be seen as needing more "seasoning." But long tenure in the same position doesn't speak well either. In some organizations there is a window of promotion opportunity that

brightens once you "pay your dues" but then begins to dim when your years in service get too advanced.

7. **How old are you relative to your contemporaries?**
   Generally speaking, if you haven't made it by the age of _____ (fill in the blank based on your job/profession/company), you're not going to. If most of the people at your level in the organization are younger than you, a promotion may be less than likely.

8. **What is your salary relative to your contemporaries?**
   Salary can be a two-faced indicator of promotability. If you make less than your peers, the message may be that you are less valued by top management. If you make much more than your peers, a promotion that might raise your salary even further could look unattractive to superiors.

9. **Do you get your share of training and development opportunities?**
   If you go to conferences and management development programs more often than your peers, it's probably not because your boss thinks you need more help. Being chosen to go to such events is a reward for performance, a vote of confidence, and an indicator of future promotability. (131, 132)

10. **How well are you known both inside and outside the company?**
    It's not *what* you know, nor is it *whom* you know—it's *who knows you.* The more people who know your accomplishments and reputation for quality performance, the more likely that you will be "discovered." (133)

11. **How powerful is your boss?**
    Got a weak boss with little clout in the organization? You're probably not going anywhere, short of replacing him or her. By contrast, a powerful boss who has the ear of top management can represent you well

throughout the hierarchy and keep your name and accomplishments in front of the right people. (140)

#130
Fourteen Tips on Preparing a Résumé

1. **Keep it short and simple.**
   You're not writing an autobiography; you're summarizing the highlights of your professional career. Say what's most important for your reader to know. Report your accomplishments and background in the fewest number of words. Use short sentences. Have it edited for conciseness. Create a one-page version for situations where brevity will be appreciated, and a longer version (2–3 pages) when more detail is needed.

2. **Make it attractive.**
   The moment your résumé is seen by a recruiter it must say, "I represent a professional." Stay away from gimmicks; stick with class and quality. Use standard size paper (8 1/2 × 11 inches) of high quality bond in white, off-white, or conservative pastel color. Have it typeset or run off on a laser printer. Stick with black ink. Consider modest use of newsletter graphics to improve eye appeal.

3. **Do not include a business card or photograph.**
   These make you look pretentious.

4. **Center your name, address, and phone number at the top.**
   This helps to identify your résumé when it's lying on a desk. Other personal data such as age, marital status, physical characteristics, social security number, religion, and citizenship are rarely included. They tend to hurt more than help.

5. **Write a short statement of your career objective.**
   Tell the recruiter the type of job and organization you

are looking for in one to three sentences. "To work in human resource training and development in an aggressive manufacturing company." If you can be more specific, such as, "To train midlevel managers in leadership skills in an aggressive manufacturing company," you'll look more sure about what you want. The trade-off is that you might close a door that you would have rather had the chance to walk through.

6. **Develop the sections of your résumé along functional categories.**

   The standard résumé categories are a selection of the following:

   A. Education*
   B. Special Training
   C. Professional Areas of Interest
   D. Languages
   E. Experience*
   F. Abilities and Accomplishments
   G. Publications and Speeches
   H. Honors and Awards
   I. Professional Associations
   J. Personal Information
   K. References

   Those which are starred are most important. Include other categories only if you are strong in them and the company where you are applying prizes them. Limit yourself to five to eight categories, organized to emphasize your strengths and minimize your weaknesses.

7. **Under Education list degrees, institutions, and dates of attendance, with the most recent school (highest degree) first.**

   In certain cases, it may be a good idea to list courses that were particularly relevant to the desired job. Otherwise, describe only work that led to a degree, certificate, or professional accreditation. Don't hesitate to highlight a liberal arts degree. It is increasingly recog-

SAMPLE RÉSUMÉ

Jamie G. Benjamin
628 North Highland Avenue
Franklin, Ohio 12345
412-555-2468

CAREER OBJECTIVES	To be a management development trainer in a *Fortune* 500 company, with a specialization in leadership, interpersonal relations, and presentation skills.
EDUCATION	Master of Business Administration, 1987, Central State University (Concentration in Human Relations). Bachelor of Science in Industrial Engineering, 1985, Sandy Creek College.
SPECIAL TRAINING	Train the Trainers Workshop, 1995. Two week institute conducted by U.S. Training Laboratories. Management Development Today, 1996. Four day seminar offered by Midwest University.
LANGUAGES	SPANISH: Reading and speaking proficiency, excellent. ARABIC: Speaking proficiency, good.
EXPERIENCE	1988–Present: Powers Manufacturing Company, Stowe, Ohio Hired as shop supervisor. Promoted to section manager in 1991 and to human resources specialist in 1994. Promoted to vice president for human resources in 1997. In 1996 chaired task force that reorganized the Human Resources Department. Designed and conducted following management training programs. * Managing for Quality Outcomes * Running Effective Meetings * Executive Presentation Skills * Managing Organizational Conflict
PROFESSIONAL MEMBERSHIPS	American Society of Training Directors, Midwest Regional Treasurer, 1996 American Association of Human Resource Managers

nized that today's executive needs to be well-rounded in order to succeed.

8. **Under Experience list employers, job titles, and dates of employment in chronological order.**

Include any job related to your career objective, even if it was part time or voluntary. Show any progression you made from jobs of lesser to greater responsibility. You may wish to list your most significant accomplishments on each job, especially those you can quantify through numbers, in lieu of a separate section on Abilities and Accomplishments. If you have embarrassing gaps of unemployment, don't highlight them by showing exact dates (to the month) at each job.

9. **Under Abilities and Accomplishments list specific, measurable achievements related to your career goals.**

Describe your accomplishments with action words such as *designed, directed, reduced, simplified, established.* Highlight what you actually accomplished, not what you have the potential to accomplish. Rather than saying, "I can effectively manage a budget," say "Reduced manpower budget by 10% while increasing productivity 15%." List accomplishments associated with each of the jobs listed under Experience.

10. **If you have written articles or made presentations, include a Publications and Speeches section.**

Communication skills are in short supply in the business world. Recruiters are impressed by candidates who can document them.

11. **If you decide against a References section, don't write "References are available upon request."**

Prospective employers don't have to be told that they can ask for your references. If you are going to list names, be certain you have up-to-date telephone numbers and mailing addresses. Never list a reference without first asking that person, "Will you feel comfortable giving me a positive recommendation for a job in . . . ?" Don't include a reference who will condemn you with faint praise.

12. **Write at least two résumés.**

Create a traditional one using these guidelines and a nontraditional one that reflects your personal style. Change the order of categories, be boastful, choose a wild color, type it on an old typewriter, include unexpected information, or do something else that strikes you. Use this version when your instincts tell you it will get attention. Experiment with it, and try to get feedback. Create distinct editions of your résumé for recruiters in different industries, different parts of the country, or in other settings with slightly altered emphases.

13. **Have two people proofread the finished copy.**

Don't bother with people who aren't good proofreaders, or who won't be critical. Never send out a résumé that has a typo or misspelled word or carries a tone you don't want it to have.

14. **Write a cover letter.**

Never send a résumé without a brief cover letter. Address it by name to the person you wish to read it. State that you are interested in making a change, why, and when. Put no negative statements in the letter; be upbeat. End by saying what you want the other person to do: "I am available for an interview at your convenience and look forward to hearing from you."

#131
*Seven Guidelines for Selecting
Training Programs That Will
Enhance Your Effectiveness*

1. **Determine the specific job-related benefits you and your people will derive.**

Move beyond the stated training objectives and examine the claimed benefits of the program. Is this what you need?

2. **Talk to trusted colleagues who have attended the program.**
   Did they gain valuable tools they apply to their jobs?

3. **Personally talk to the session leader.**
   Get a feel for his or her philosophy. Do you think you could enjoy listening to this person for the full length of the program?

4. **Check the qualifications of the organization sponsoring the training and the person conducting it.**
   What are their reputations in the field? (105)

5. **Be wary of courses that promise too much.**
   Do they claim more benefits than they can possibly deliver?

6. **Ask how many participants they expect.**
   Seminars that enroll more than 50 people typically do not provide for questions or other substantive interaction between the leader and participants. This is normally the case when the registration fee is low.

7. **Consider the cost of a specialized session.**
   If you're planning to send several participants to a seminar, it may make more sense to bring the trainer into your company, where even more employees can attend for what may be an insignificant marginal cost.

#132
Twelve Steps for Translating Training into Improved Performance

1. **Select the right training program.** (130)
2. **Find out as much as you can about the program before you go.**
   Read a book by the leader, talk to previous participants, write for an advance outline or reading materi-

als. The idea is to begin thinking about—and perhaps even begin using—program concepts before the training begins.

3. **Set goals.**

   Develop a list of three to six overall goals to focus yourself on the potential value of the experience. These goals should be oriented toward skill acquisition, quality improvement, sales increase, cost reduction, or enhanced profit.

4. **Get to the session early; meet the leader.**

   Communicate your interest in the program. Generate the leader's interest in you.

5. **Sit near the front.**

   You'll get more involved and you'll hear better.

6. **Ask questions and make comments.**

   You'll become immersed in the topic, and the direction taken by the leader will reflect your interests more fully. Come to the session knowing specific questions you'll want answered.

7. **Leave your work responsibilities in good hands.**

   Once the program begins, concentrate on it and not on work.

8. **Don't call your office; tell them not to call you.**

   You will cheat yourself and your company if you attempt to conduct business while training. Even your evenings should be free to reflect on the learning experience.

9. **Think about what you are learning rather than trying to write it down.**

   Taking notes will be useful, but should not interfere with your listening and learning. Don't return home with volumes of useless reference notes. Just record the "gems" that you want to document. The goal is to fill your head, not your library. (5)

10. **Network with colleagues during free time.**

    You can sometimes gain as much for your company

and yourself at breaks and meals as during the training itself. (134)

11. **Write a personal action plan for what you are going to do differently as a result of the program.**
Hold yourself accountable for translating learning into performance. (111)

12. **Back on the job, share your new insights with subordinates, peers, and superiors.**
Expect some resistance, disbelief, and misunderstanding; proceed sensitively and carefully. Put into writing the most important insights you wish to share with them. You may want to write a three-page report based on your action plan and notes, and circulate it to "anyone who might be interested."

#133
Ten Steps for Increasing Your Visibility in the Company

1. **Outperform your competition.**
Make sure everything you do in the company is done on time, under budget, to company requirements, and with pride.

2. **Get your boss to take you to meetings with his or her peers.**
Make eye contact and speak to them if possible, but do not be intrusive or overbearing.

3. **Volunteer for projects that have high visibility.**
These are also likely to be the projects with greater risks for failure. But with risk comes reward.

4. **Work on in-house, philanthropic causes.**
Seek particular involvement in favorites of top management, such as the United Way, Scouts, and other charities.

5. **Find out what's happening in other departments.**
   Make a point of tracking major projects outside your department. Be sure the work of your department supports and complements these projects.

6. **Remember the names of key executives.**
   Greet them by name when you see them in the cafeteria, parking lot, or hallway. (128)

7. **Learn the political ropes of your company.**
   Who controls the grapevine? Who are the unofficial task leaders in each department? How does one succeed here?

8. **Write articles for the company newsletter.**
   Even if they're only on topics such as your hobby, some senior officer is likely to read the article and identify with your interests or views. (27, 28)

9. **Get your name on companywide reports.**
   Whenever you publish a report, give everyone due credit, especially yourself.

10. **Sharpen your presentation skills.**
    Find an opportunity to wow top management with them. (11–26)

#134
Twelve Strategies for Networking

1. **Collect business cards, distribute yours.**
2. **Write notes on the back of each card.**
   Remind yourself of where and when you met the person and what you want to remember about him or her.
3. **Read the trade publication for your industry.**
   Monitor job placement in your industry. Who are the names in the news?
4. **Try to attend a trade show or professional conference at least once a year.**
   Meet as many people as you can.

5. **Drop personal notes to colleagues who have achieved recognition.**
6. **Become active in civic or professional groups.**
7. **Serve on committees and task forces.**
   Especially those with high visibility in the organization.
8. **Have lunch with colleagues outside your company at least once a month.**
9. **If you're a line manager, make friends with a staff manager, and vice versa.**
10. **Keep your personal telephone directory and mailing list up to date.**
11. **When you change jobs, spread the word.**
12. **Get friendly with the editor of the company newsletter.**
    You'll be written up in it frequently.

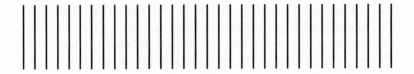

14. Manage Your Boss

CARTOONS are a powerful communication medium. Through their humor they point out the foibles, hypocrisies, pet peeves, and pretensions we all recognize but are reluctant to discuss. They represent "society's ombudsman"—a safe way to air the grievances we would otherwise conceal.

Scan a sample of popular magazines or daily newspapers and you'll see a significant portion of cartoons dealing with boss-subordinate relationships. It would appear as if American cartoonists are allowing us to vent our frustration with our bosses through laughter—a release far safer than one which many of us may fantasize about.

The reason why frustration with bosses is such a "hot topic" for cartoonists is easily understood. Aside from your parents and your spouse, there is probably no other adult relationship with the potential to make your day-to-day life a living heaven or a living hell.

Who is the most important person in determining your upward mobility? Your boss. Who has control over your raises and bonuses? Your boss. Who has direct authority in assigning you jobs that enhance your skills and self-esteem versus those that dehumanize you into a robot? Your boss. What is a major potential cause of psychosomatic illnesses? Your boss.

On a day-to-day basis your boss has direct control over your career and your earning power, and thus indirect effect on your self-concept. In short, bosses have the potential to enhance our lives or to make us sick.

Our experience as executive coaches convinces us that there are many more bosses who depress their subordinates than there are who lift their subordinates up. We are further convinced that subordinates have far greater control in their relationship with their bosses than they typically realize.

Invariably someone in one of our workshops will say something like, "Gee, this is really great stuff, but the person who really needs to hear it isn't in this room. You guys ought to be giving this workshop for my boss."

Our response is swift and direct. "Right now the only person in this room is you. Forget about changing your boss. Worry about changing you and the way you relate to your boss and you may discover that your boss has changed."

We offer you the same advice. Don't worry if your boss hasn't read this book (although we think all bosses should). You can't control or change your boss. It's futile even to try. The only person you can change is you. The only part of your relationship with your boss that you can change is that part which you control. But when you have changed how you relate to your boss, you will discover that your boss has changed.

You need not be at the mercy of someone you describe as a cross between Attila the Hun and J. R. Ewing. Bosses aren't destined to be autocratic despots; indeed, they are often surprised to discover they are perceived that way. And subordinates are not destined to be spineless sycophants.

Study the lists and begin relating to your boss differently. When you do, you will discover that the next time you see a cartoon depicting the pathos in boss-subordinate relationships, you will laugh just because it's funny—not because it hits close to home.

#135

Fourteen Steps to Keep Any Boss Happy

1. **Be very good at what you do.**
   Make certain everything you do is done on time, under budget, to requirements, and with pride of craftsmanship.

2. **Be a successful leader.**
   Keep your people happy, productive, and out of your boss's hair. (36–47)

3. **Save your organization money.**
   Every boss at every level is under a constant mandate to conserve resources. Your help reducing expenses will be remembered.

4. **Make money for your organization.**
   You are probably in a better position than anyone else to see unrealized income potential in your sector of the organization. Make a feasible suggestion for seizing that potential and your boss will love you.

5. **Learn what's really important to your boss.**
   Show by your actions that those same things are important to you.

6. **Learn your boss's expectations of you.**
   Not all bosses are direct and specific in stating their expectations. All the same, they expect you to meet those expectations. If you have any doubts, find out without implying the boss is derelict for not telling you. "Am I giving you enough detail on my monthly report?" is better than, "I'm not sure what you expect on my monthly report." (71)

7. **Get feedback on your performance.**
   Find out how well you're doing. Some bosses withhold praise—perhaps because you don't accept it graciously. Others aren't free with criticism—perhaps because you become defensive too easily. Ask for

feedback on your work without making the boss uncomfortable and without making yourself look insecure. (138)

8. **See that most problems are solved before they come to the boss's attention.**

   But don't overstep the limits of discretion you are given.

9. **See that both bad news and good news come from you.**

   Keep the boss as closely informed as he or she wants to be on matters of your responsibility. Do not make the boss be surprised by news from a third party. That makes both of you look bad.

10. **Volunteer for difficult and unwanted assignments.**

    You win points whenever you step forward to get your boss off the hook. And when you succeed where no one else can, you are tagged as a rising star.

11. **Sell only worthwhile ideas.**

    If your boss has to turn down most of your requests and suggestions, you could look like a scatterbrain. The secret to success in selling ideas to your boss is to show how your idea will either improve the bottom line or make the boss look good. If your idea does neither, it's not a worthwhile idea. (82)

12. **Don't ask for unnecessary guidance.**

    Many bosses would rather be informed of what you plan to do, with an opportunity for redirecting your plan, than to be given options to choose from. It is often better to write, "This is my plan for the fall training schedule; unless I hear from you by Friday, I'll send it to the printer," than, "Let me know by Friday which of these training schedules you favor."

13. **Don't complain about other people.**

    When things go wrong accept your share of the responsibility, and don't lay blame at the feet of others. But even more than an admission of error, most superiors are looking for assurance that it won't happen again.

14. **Be a tough self-critic.**

    Your boss is not going to tell you all the things wrong with your performance. You'll have to discover some of them on your own. Be aware of yourself. Look intently for both verbal and nonverbal feedback from the boss and others. Always work at cleaning up your act.

#136

Nine Smart Ways to Communicate with Your Boss

1. **Provide a context for your messages.**

   Bosses are busy people, usually with more than one subordinate. Don't expect your boss to be up on every development in your area. Begin every important briefing with something like, "I am facing a Friday deadline on the training plan for the XYZ Division. Last week you had asked me to revise the section on communication skills to reflect more of an interpersonal thrust. This is what I've come up with."

2. **Be direct, crisp, and brief.**

   Bosses don't want to play guessing games with you. Use plain language. Economize on words. Organize your presentation; throw out the unnecessary. But don't appear rushed or curt when you speak. (3)

3. **Anticipate questions and needs for information.**

   The best briefings will answer most questions. If you have been studying your boss, you know the direction his or her line of questioning is likely to take. Be prepared with the answers and you'll look great.

4. **Learn the boss's style of writing and relating to others.**

   Imitate these when acting (especially when writing)

on his or her behalf. Before long the boss will be signing letters you draft without even reading them.

5. **Accept criticism in stride.**

   Don't become defensive; rather, show a desire to use the feedback to improve your effectiveness. If you react poorly to criticism, it may be withheld until it's too late or until it builds into a hurricane of reaction. (138)

6. **Take praise well.**

   Accept praise that you have earned without showing false modesty or negating the gift of praise. A simple "thank you" is what's called for.

7. **Correct your boss with tact.**

   But don't challenge, threaten, or criticize. Don't say, "You're wrong about . . . ," when you can say, "I wonder if we shouldn't take another look at the [not "your"] decision to . . ." Disagree, but don't dispute. (45, 46)

8. **Praise, but don't flatter.**

   Bosses need an occasional pat on the back. When something the boss engineered has worked out well, don't be afraid to say so. ("The decision to hire a PR manager has been instrumental in improving our dealings with the press.") However, avoid platitudes. ("Your idea to hire a PR manager is further evidence to me of why you're the boss.")

9. **Don't offer unsolicited promises to gain favor.**

   A promise is an invitation to failure. Besides, delivery of excellence is more powerful when it has not been discounted in advance by a promise of delivery.

#137

Nine Suggestions on Asking for a Raise

1. **Time the request to coincide with one of your major accomplishments.**

2. **Time the request to coincide with your company's success.**

3. **Time the request to coincide with one of your boss's better moods.**

4. **Do your homework.**
   What do comparable professionals in your company or industry earn? Cite the source. If this analysis is not favorable, you won't draw attention to it, but if your boss does, have a plan for overcoming this objection. (81)

5. **Plan the request as a "sales call" on your boss.**
   Sell your proposal and be prepared to overcome the objections your boss is most likely to have. (82–84)

6. **Put yourself in your boss's shoes.**
   If you were the boss what would you say to the request? What are the reasons why he or she might say no? Answer these objections in your presentation.

7. **How is granting you a raise in your boss's best interest?**
   If you can't come up with a good answer to this question, don't waste your time asking for a raise.

8. **Justify your request with specific data that links your performance to company success.**
   Maintain a log and file of materials that document your accomplishments. Hard data is difficult to dismiss.

9. **Don't threaten resignation or mention other offers unless you are prepared to leave.**

#138
Ten Tips for Handling Criticism

1. **Try not to get angry.**
   The remaining suggestions on this list will be impossible if you lose your temper. It's not easy to keep cool.

It requires self esteem, a sincere belief that everyone is entitled to an opinion, and a powerful desire to rid yourself of anger and frustration. (77)

2. **Listen intently to the criticism.**

Understand exactly what is being said and why, so you can respond appropriately later. If nothing else, you will learn a lot by hearing this person out fully. You will also cause the person to feel better about you. No matter how difficult, say nothing until the criticizer is finished or asks you a question. (5)

3. **Pity inept criticizers.**

If criticism is given ineptly or punitively, it is better to focus your attention on the inability of the giver than to feel injured. Imagine the other poor people who may also have to suffer from this unenlightened person. Don't attribute to malice what can be explained by incompetence.

4. **Ask for examples of your alleged shortcomings.**

Do this with a genuine desire to get to the bottom of the person's claims. Don't be sarcastic or antagonistic. Ask whatever questions might help you understand the situation, showing your desire to hear the person out.

5. **Share _your_ perceptions of the situation.**

First, acknowledge the extent of your agreement with the comments. Politely, yet firmly, correct any inaccurate information held by the criticizer. Treat the issues as dispassionately as you can.

6. **Never accuse the criticizer of being unfair.**

Even though you may think the criticism is unfair, you can be certain the critic doesn't think so. You may eventually be able to get people to see the error of their ways, but not by accusing them. (45, 46)

7. **Summarize your disagreement.**

Point out the remaining discrepancies between your

two views in specific terms. Assert your position firmly, but without malice. Suggest corrective action to resolve the remaining disagreement.

8. **State your feelings.**

   Once the issues have been dealt with, describe your feelings about the criticism as you received it. Provide feedback to the giver on how you think he or she might do better.

9. **Thank the criticizer.**

   Show appreciation for his or her desire to help you improve your performance, even though you may not feel helped.

10. **Implement agreed-to corrective actions.**

    Change behaviors that led to valid criticisms. Be certain the criticizer sees those changes.

#139

Ten Tips for the Mentor-Protégé Relationship

1. **If your mentor or protégé is of the opposite sex, recognize that decorum, professionalism, and discretion are paramount.**

   People will talk. Make sure they have nothing to talk about.

2. **Don't force the relationship.**

   Let it evolve naturally over time.

3. **Be true to your mentor or protégé.**

   Give public support. "Run interference" when necessary.

4. **Recognize the potential drawbacks of the relationship.**

   Each may expect things from the other party which

the other may not be able to give. Build the relationship, but also maintain your individuality.

5. **Make your expectations explicit.**
   Don't expect the other person to read your mind; let your needs be known. (71)

6. **Give each other feedback on how well the relationship is meeting your needs.**
   Regardless how difficult and painful it might be, tell the other party what you're feeling and why. (45)

7. **If you're the protégé, don't feel guilty because your peers weren't chosen.**
   You have no reason to feel guilty. But don't flaunt or abuse the relationship.

8. **If you're the mentor, don't discriminate against other people on your team.**
   Even though one subordinate is favored, all must be treated equally if teamwork is to be maintained.

9. **If you're the protégé, make sure you perform.**
   Your mentor has probably gone out on a limb for you. Don't saw it off.

10. **If you're the mentor, don't jeopardize your standing by supporting a protégé who doesn't deliver.**
    Link up with competent workers, not just people you like.

#140

Ten Things to Do If Your Boss Is a Jerk

1. **Stop expecting more than the boss can deliver.**
   If you have no expectations, you'll never be disappointed. (71)

2. **View the objectionable behavior as the boss's problem, not yours.**

3. **Never attribute to malice what can be explained by incompetence.**

   Contrary to appearance, malice is at work only a very small part of the time. The usual reasons for seemingly arbitrary and capricious decisions are lack of information, insensitivity, and stupidity. Don't give any more credit for cunning than people deserve.

4. **Spend more time with subordinates and less time with your boss.**

   It will be more satisfying to you, and you should anyway.

5. **Confront your boss in private.**

   Initiate the discussion you've always wanted to have. But do this carefully. Ask your boss what the two of you can do to make your relationship more productive and the organization more successful.

6. **Try a joint feedback session.**

   If your boss agrees, write three headings on a blank sheet of paper: "Do more of," "Do less of," and "Keep the same." Under each of those headings write behaviors of *yours* that you believe the boss would put in those categories for *you*. Have your boss do the same by writing behaviors he or she believes you would place in those categories for him or her. Each of you will look at the other's self-attributed behaviors and say what you agree with, disagree with, and would like to add. The most important ground rule in the exercise is that each of you must select three behaviors from your final list that you commit to changing immediately in order to improve the relationship.

7. **Keep your outside options open in case you choose to quit.**

   Remain visible in the organization and in your profession. Keep your résumé up to date.

8. **Outlast the boss and wait for a better replacement.**

9. Your good work may eventually get you promoted into the job now held by the boss.
10. When all else fails, polish up the boss's résumé and send it to a search firm.

ACTION INDEX

SMART *MOVES* enables you to solve problems and meet needs in your job. The index below provides an immediate reference to the advice you need to carry out 40 of the most challenging management tasks.

Ask for a raise	Same as #19 plus 135–137
Go to a training program	5, 131, 132
Provide training to subordinates	98, 106, 107, 131, 132
Improve the relationship with your boss	3, 5, 135–140
Hire a consultant	90, 92, 94, 95, 105, 114
Implement a merit pay program	52, 54, 82–84, 98, 114
Establish quality circles	57, 59–66, 115, 117, 122
Reduce your stress	16, 27, 70, 72, 77, 78, 80
Negotiate an agreement	3, 5, 8, 81–86
Get more information from subordinates	5, 24, 39, 56, 68, 91, 92, 96, 98, 103, 116
Empower subordinates	5, 37–39, 42, 43, 51, 55, 57, 65, 101, 102, 107, 131, 132
Deal with employee substance abuse	3, 5, 39, 44–47, 109
Terminate an employee	3, 6, 11, 44, 75–77, 83, 84, 110
Formulate a strategic plan	11, 29, 50, 111–113
Make a decision	5, 58, 114–117, 125
Analyze a problem	44, 114–117, 125
Enhance your career	2, 3, 5, 10, 67, 80, 82–84, 97, 118–140
Deal with difficult people	25, 44–47, 62, 63, 70–78, 80–86, 104, 109, 110, 116, 140
Make a good impression	5, 28, 88, 126–128, 130, 135, 136
Introduce a speaker	3, 5, 12, 15–18, 20–22, 26
Increase your self-awareness	2, 5, 8, 10, 68, 69, 71, 77, 80, 138

ABOUT THE AUTHORS

Sam Deep taught at the college level for twenty years, most recently in the Communication Department of the University of Pittsburgh, where he also served as an administrator. In 1985 he turned his part-time consulting practice into a full-time career. He now helps organizations empower employees by enhancing the interpersonal, communication, and leadership skills of their managers.

Lyle Sussman is Professor of Management in the School of Business, University of Louisville, Kentucky. Previously he was affiliated with the University of Michigan and the University of Pittsburgh. He received his Ph.D. in Communications and Industrial Relations from Purdue University.

Deep and Sussman conduct seminars and give speeches for a variety of organizations from the *Fortune* 500, the health industry, public school systems, colleges and universities, professional associations, and government agencies. Their clients include Alcoa, the American Bankers Association, the American Institute of Banking, the Austrian National Bank, Bayer, Deloitte & Touche, General Electric, Hallmark Cards, Humana, Kentucky Fried Chicken, Kraft Foods, the National Cattleman's Association, PPG, Rally's Hamburgers, Rockwell International, Sandler Sales Institute, and the University of Texas.

Among their most requested programs are Achieving Exceptional Customer Service, Building and Sustaining High Performance Work Teams, Communicating with Confidence, Dealing With Difficult People—What to Say to Get What You Want, Getting from Yesterday to Tomorrow—Helping Change Happen, Make It Happen!—The Teamwork Challenge, Making Meetings Work, Managing Conflict, Anger, and Hostility, Presenting Yourself With Impact, Selling Your Ideas to Others, Seven Secrets of Highly Effective CEOs, The Steel Spiked Servant—Leading into the Next Millennium, Successful Supervision—Leading High Performance Work Teams, Twelve Keys to Personal and Professional Success, You're Not Listening. For more information on any of these programs, audiotapes, videotapes, and other training materials, please contact:

Seminars by Sam Deep
1920 Woodside Road
Glenshaw, PA 15116
(800) 526-5869

Other Books by the Authors

Power Tools: 33 Management Inventions You Can Use Today

Yes, You Can! Twelve Hundred Inspiring Ideas for Work, Home, and Happiness

Smart Moves for People in Charge: 130 Checklists to Help You Be a Better Leader

What to Say to Get What You Want: Strong Words for 44 Challenging Bosses, Employees, Coworkers, and Customers

What to Ask When You Don't Know What to Say: 555 Powerful Questions to Use for Getting Your Way at Work

COMEX: The Communication Experience in Human Relations

Speaking Skills for Bankers

by Sam Deep

Human Relations in Management

A Program of Exercises for Management and Organizational Behavior, with James A. Vaughan

Introduction to Business: A Systems Approach, with William D. Brinkloe

Studies in Organizational Psychology, with Bernard M. Bass

Current Perspectives for Managing Organizations, with Bernard M. Bass

by Lyle Sussman

Communications for Supervisors and Managers

Increasing Supervisory Effectiveness